A Common Policy for Education

MARY WARNOCK

Oxford   New York
OXFORD UNIVERSITY PRESS
1989

Oxford University Press, Walton Street, Oxford OX2 6DP

Oxford New York Toronto
Delhi Bombay Calcutta Madras Karachi
Petaling Jaya Singapore Hong Kong Tokyo
Nairobi Dar es Salaam Cape Town
Melbourne Auckland

and associated companies in
Berlin Ibadan

Oxford is a trade mark of Oxford University Press

First published 1988 by Oxford University Press
First issued as an Oxford University Press paperback 1989

British Library Cataloguing in Publication Data

Warnock, Mary
A common policy for education.
1. Great Britain. Education. Policies of
government
I. Title
379.41

ISBN 0–19–282585–2

Library of Congress Cataloging in Publication Data

Warnock, Mary.
A common policy for education.
Bibliography: p.
Includes index.
1. Education and state—Great Britain.
2. Education—Great Britain—Aims and objectives.
I. Title.
[LC93.G7W27 1989]   370'.941   88–25322

ISBN 0–19–282585–2 (pbk.)

Printed in Great Britain by
The Guernsey Press Co. Ltd.
Guernsey, Channel Islands

Contents

Abbreviations

BTEC	Business and Technical Education Council
CGLI	City and Guilds of London Institute
CNAA	Council for National Academic Awards
CPVE	Certificate of Pre-vocational Education
CTC	City Technology Colleges
DES	Department of Education and Science
GCSE	General Certificate of Secondary Education
ILEA	Inner London Education Authority
LEA	Local Education Authority
MIT	Massachusetts Institute of Technology
MSC	Manpower Services Commission
NAB	National Advisory Body
PCFC	Polytechnic and Colleges Funding Council
PGCE	Postgraduate Certificate of Education
RE	Religious Education
RSA	Royal Society of Arts
SEC	Secondary Examinations Council
TVEI	Technical Vocational Education Initiative
UFC	Universities Funding Council
UGC	University Grants Committee

Introduction: the past

1

All children, whatever their abilities or disabilities, have a statutory right to be educated; and all parents have a corresponding duty to see that they are educated, at least up to the age of 16. To this extent Great Britain is an 'advanced' country. Education is recognized, in law, to be essential to life. But we are bound to ask what is supposed to be essential about it. No one will die from lack of education as he will from lack of food or basic health care. It seems that education is not even essential to happiness. More than a century ago J. S. Mill argued for universal education on moral grounds, holding that it would manifestly increase the general balance of pleasure over pain, happiness over unhappiness. We find today that, on the whole, universal provision has had no such effect. There are even those who look back nostalgically to the days when people might leave school at 11, when the educated classes were distinct from the uneducated. Why, then, do we make it compulsory to be educated? Why do we spend such vast amounts of money on the service? Why do we take it for granted that education is a good to which everyone equally is entitled?

If we could state positively, and with hope of agreement, what the point of education is, then we could go on to debate how it should be provided, how much public money should be spent on provision, and how much variety should be permitted, within the general legal framework. But it is precisely on the global aims, the actual purpose of education, that agreement seems impossible. Yet, paradoxically, despite a failure to agree about what education should aim for, what it should actually *do*, everyone seems to be certain both that it should do *something*, and that it is not doing it. The 'Great Debate', initiated by James Callaghan in 1977, was set up on the premise that education was failing.

The debate was mainly about what should be provided, what deficiencies should be remedied, and, to a much lesser extent, about how this should be brought about. The centre of the discussion was the school curriculum; and it was frequently observed at the time that this was the first occasion on which politicians or the public at large had concerned themselves with what had hitherto been a wholly professional matter. The curriculum had been debated, if at all, by Local Education Authorities, teachers, and the largely teacher-dominated Schools Council, as well as by the Examination Boards, over which the universities exercised the greatest influence, but never by ministers or the general public.

It is certainly true that at the time of the Butler Education Act the school curriculum was not much discussed in public, although certain assumptions about its content were in fact incorporated in the Act. It was taken for granted that education was beneficial to those who received it, and that its universal provision was one of the great social improvements that were to mark the end of the war. But what its content should be was left at first to the experts. The guiding assumption was that the school curriculum should differ according to the ability of the child who would follow it. Before the war grammar schools were distinguished by their academic curriculum, by the existence of sixth forms, from which there could be progress to university, and by the academic qualifications of the teachers; and so, after 1944, it was taken for granted that the grammar school ideal must be preserved in its familiar form. The matter for debate was what other schools there should be, and what they should teach. In the event, a tripartite system was decided on. After common primary schooling, children were selected by intelligence tests either for one of the old grammar schools or for a technical school, or for a secondary modern school. A vast building programme began, to accommodate all children from 11 to 15, and later to 16. There were not only extra years of schooling to cope with, but an increase in the birth-rate, following the war. It was a formidable and extremely expensive task.

It is worth noticing that at least one senior member of the Board of Education (William Cleary, Head of the Elementary

Branch) had argued, as early as 1941, against the tripartite system and in favour of comprehensive schools. He held that 'the obvious and perhaps the only satisfactory solution' was a multilateral post-primary school attended by all children alike. Only such a school would provide a truly democratic education, and thus assert the values for which the world war was being fought. It is interesting to speculate what the consequences would have been for the curriculum if his view had prevailed. But the practical difficulty of moving towards such a solution, given existing comparatively small school buildings, was conclusive; and the then Permanent Secretary, Maurice Holmes, advised the Minister to divide secondary school children up into relatively small units, each with its own type of curriculum, according to ability. The technical schools, where they were established, were, on the whole, short-lived. By the 1950s practically all maintained secondary schools were either grammar schools or modern schools.

Section 1 of the 1944 Act gave tremendous responsibilities to the Minister: 'It shall be the duty of the Minister of Education to promote the education of the people of England and Wales and the progressive development of institutions devoted to that purpose, and to secure the effective execution by Local Authorities, under his control and direction, of national policy for providing a comprehensive educational service in every area.' Central government was to determine policy; LEAs were to provide what was required. But it should not be thought that at this time the Minister relied solely on the advice of his civil servants for the formation of policy. Education Committees, which were a statutory part of every Local Authority, were extremely influential through their joint body, the Association of Education Committees. It was they who caused a reluctant minister to accept, in 1963, the introduction of an examination at 15 + other than O level (the CSE examination) specifically designed for the next 40 per cent of the ability range below the 20 per cent for whom O level was thought to be appropriate. It was they, with the largest of the teachers' unions, the NUT, who were largely responsible for the establishment of the Schools Council, to advise and experiment in respect of curricular content.

The Schools Council has now been abolished, and so has the Association of Education Committees. The teaching profession is in disarray, speaking with no coherent voice. Almost everyone concerned with education is looking for the right direction to go, and there is much talk of leadership. What should be taught and to whom? These are still the central questions, more than ten years after the Great Debate. In order to understand our present confusion it is necessary once again to go back to its history. Only so can we begin to examine the contradictory presuppositions of educational theory, conceptual confusions which have led inevitably to fumbling and uncertain practice.

In 1944, as we have seen, it was presumed that the best minds must be educated in the way that was traditional, by means of the grammar school curriculum, based originally on the classics and mathematics, gradually expanded, before the war, to include modern languages and experimental sciences. It was taken for granted, as we have also seen, that education was a social benefit, and therefore, in the new post-war democracy, something to which everyone was entitled. Thus the growth of secondary education was a development parallel to that of the National Health Service. But, like the National Health Service, education could be seen in a different light. It was not only a personal benefit, but a social and economic necessity. A society consisting of educated people, like a society of healthy people, made economic sense. Education was a necessity if the country was to recover from the industrial and commercial effects of war. The great expenditure on education could be justified as a means to a thoroughly acceptable common end: economic growth. Personal and national interests seemed to coincide. But gradually in the 1950s and 1960s it became clear that, though the economy had grown considerably since 1945, the UK was not keeping up with its rivals abroad. Faith in education as an instrument of growth began to be eroded, and increasingly it came to be regarded, especially by the Treasury, as an extravagant indulgence.

Meanwhile the notion of education as an instrument, or means to an end, was subject to pressures of a quite different kind. The 1960s were, as we can see now, in some ways rightly to be thought of as a time of indulgence. Rhetorically, it was the time of the great horticultural images of education, derived perhaps first from Rousseau and reinforced by Froebel, for whom the child was the tender plant growing in the garden, the kindergarten. School was the garden where children must grow and flourish. Throughout the sixties and well into the seventies, children were *cultivated* at school, not taught. The Plowden Report on primary school education, *Children and their Primary Schools* (1967), was immensely influential. Just as a gardener is concerned first and foremost with his plants, so, according to Plowden, 'At the heart of every educational process lies the child.'[1] And the report continues to urge that the main method of educational reform should be 'deliberately to devise the right environment for children, to allow them to be themselves, and to develop in the way and at the pace appropriate to them'.[2] Above all, the educational theories of the American philosopher John Dewey, belatedly crossing the Atlantic, held sway, especially in teacher-training colleges.

Dewey saw that there was a potential conflict between the ideal of education as an instrument and that of education as self-development, but he could not believe that such equally desirable ideals could ultimately be in contradiction one to the other. He therefore sought to show that they were not only capable of reconciliation, but, albeit obscurely, identical. In *Democracy and Education* he argued that, whereas for the ancient Greeks self-development had consisted in contemplation and abstract 'academic' study, while work for the community was a matter of low-grade, despicable manual work, in the twentieth century this dichotomy had simply withered away. The advance of modern science had shown that science, even at its most theoretical level, is dependent on experiment, on practical doing as well as abstract thinking. Therefore the pre-Renaissance gulf between the 'pure' and the 'applied', the thought and the action, had disappeared. This is an important idea to which we shall return. But Dewey's application of it had a very direct effect on educational practice in the classroom. For he was realistic enough to recognize that even if the Greek distinction between the 'pure' and the 'useful' was ultimately illusory, still the kind of class-division to which it had given rise was deeply engrained. In order to overcome it, schools must play an active part. Instead of the old concept of teaching, according to which the teacher, possessed of superior powers and superior knowledge, attempted to pass on to the more able of his pupils that non-practical culture which would most benefit them personally, a new class-room communication should be envisaged. This was to be the communication of joint discovery and experiment. Side by side, teacher and pupil should test and render practical any theoretical ideas that were presented. Equally, by exploring the environment of the class-room, it would be open to pupils themselves to discover new scientific truths, by their own empirical means. The result would be a kind of consensus of truth, a fully democratic method of discovering what was useful, what actually worked, and thus what was true. Teacher and pupil, even primary school pupil, were equal partners in this joint exploration. The true is what works, and everyone is equally capable, in this sense, of finding the true and rejecting the false.[3]

In practice this theory led, in British primary schools, to a fashion for so-called 'discovery methods' of learning, and a strong reaction against any teaching that was imposed from above, including, especially, any kind of rote learning. What a child found out for himself was deemed to be real and usable knowledge, while what he learned 'parrot-fashion' was not. It is easy to understand the excitement that such new teaching practice could generate. The very word 'teaching' came to be looked on with disfavour, implying, as it did, an unacceptable *de-haut-en-bas* presumption with regard to the teacher's role. It was disconcerting for visitors to primary schools to see teachers, who had declined to teach their pupils the multiplication tables, hoping to get them to discover for themselves how to count up books, conveniently arranged round the room in groups of four. The longing to get them to recite their tables was almost overwhelming for the non-converted. Instead of to *teaching*, a child at school had to be exposed to *experiences*; for experiencing is learning. The formalization of learning was not only unnecessary and inhibiting, but politically divisive. Democracy of the shared class-room experience is the cradle of democracy in the outside world. Thus education was to be productive of a 'good', politically respectable State; but it must not be seen as instrumental in any narrow or vocational way.

At the same time as these theories were being explored in the world of school—theories designed to make the pupil the equal of the teacher—the concept of equality was beginning to have a powerful effect on education in a more overtly political sense.

Hugh Gaitskell, more influential as leader of the Opposition than many prime ministers, had declared that socialism was about equality. He was in favour of comprehensive schools, disliking selection once and for all for one sort of education or another at 'this frankly absurdly early age of 11 + ', and disliking also the social divisiveness of middle-class and working-class children going to different schools. This last point was, however, mainly directed towards the public schools and the independent sector generally. For comprehensive schools were still in the late 1950s regarded as experimental, and in any case suitable only for certain areas, such as rural parts of the country hitherto ill-served by grammar schools. There was still much confused thinking, at least until the early 1960s, about selection. In 1963, when he was already Leader of the Labour Party, Harold Wilson promised that under a Labour government there would be 'Grammar School education for all', and few in the Labour Party wanted to be seen as the enemy of the grammar schools. For it was still universally accepted that the academic type of education offered at such schools was the best. Indeed, the assumption among Labour 'intellectuals' such as Harold Wilson, Richard Crossman, Anthony Crosland, and Hugh Dalton was that the best possible education was at a public school even if the public schools, on political grounds, had to go. Second best were the grammar schools, deemed to be a kind of honorary public schools; secondary modern schools were not in the running. Those radicals (among whom Gaitskell was, oddly, not numbered) who wanted to abolish the public schools, or amalgamate them somehow into the maintained system, persuaded themselves for a time that if this were done, and if everyone had a chance to take the 11 + and compete for a place at a grammar school, then justice would have been done and educational standards would be secure. The nature and content of grammar school education was hardly questioned.

But gradually it began to dawn on people, not only politicians but teachers and educationalists as well, that 'grammar school for all' was an absurd idea. The grammar school was intrinsically selective, and always had been. If there was to be selection then some would inevitably be selected out of the grammar school class. There were various more or less half-hearted attempts to get over the finality of this selection. Sometimes a grammar school and a secondary modern school were located close to one another, even on the same 'campus', in order to facilitate the sharing of resources, or the movement of pupils from one to the other. Sometimes modern schools started O level and even A level classes. Later, Grade 1 of the CSE, the examination designed for modern schools, was officially deemed to be the equivalent of a pass at O level, so that pupils who had attended modern schools where only CSE was on offer could, in theory at least, compete for those further education or training opportunities that demanded a number of O level passes. But that modern schools struggled to make themselves in various ways as academic as grammar schools did not entail any real equality between the two kinds of school. Certainly 'equality of esteem', originally intended to cover all the parts of the tripartite school system, did not exist, and parents became increasingly discontented with the outcome of the 11 + , as well as with the strain and anxiety it imposed on children, primary teachers, and families.

Meanwhile the 11 + began to be criticized not only because it divided children up absurdly young into different categories, within which they were more or less trapped, but also because it was intrinsically inequitable. For it became increasingly obvious that it did not, as had been intended, miraculously detect native intelligence in children however uneducated, but, on the contrary, was strongly biased in favour of middle-class children who had larger vocabularies than their working-class contemporaries, and who were in any case accustomed to tests and examinations. A place at grammar school was seen as hardly more genuinely open to everyone than a fee-paying place at a public school; and so the move towards comprehensive schools was made, largely on grounds of justice. The 11 + was unfair and divisive. The arguments used by the radicals against the continued existence of the independent sector were now turned and used against the continued existence of grammar schools and direct grant schools (which were equally selective and even more predominantly middle-class).

Thus by the mid-1960s, under the first Wilson Government, arguments about education were almost entirely concerned with the structure of the system. In so far as any thought was given to the curriculum, this was held to be a matter for expert 'curriculum designers' who spoke in a language all their own, and seldom impinged on the consciousness of the public. In any case, O levels and A levels, examinations which were external to the schools (though administered with increasing teacher-participation) were there to maintain standards for those pupils who took them. The content of their syllabuses was largely, though indirectly, in the hands of the universities, through the local examination boards, and it was assumed that a good school, even if comprehensive, would manage to get a reasonable number of O and A level passes and send a proportion of its pupils on to higher education. The number of these passes was, and still is, widely seen as the sole criterion of 'standards' in education.

Of course there were dissentient voices. There were greater or less demands for absolute equality in different parts of the country, and in different Local Education Authorities. Some schools, in principle at least, not only admitted children of all abilities, but taught them together when they had them. Mixed-ability teaching was a principle fairly widely accepted, at least for children in their first year at secondary school, but in some schools for far longer. Those who advocated it argued that it was of no use to abolish selection at 11 +, in the name of justice and fairness, and then reintroduce selection a few months later, by streaming children once at school. A good deal of evidence was produced to show that children tend to conform to their teachers' expectations of them. Thus C stream children perform at a C stream level. Far from showing that teachers are very experienced predictors of how children will perform, this was taken to show that children will do, more or less, what is expected of them, whatever that may be. If it was pointed out that in mixed-ability classes too little was now being expected of the very clever child, teachers tended to reply that such children could look after themselves, and required, or deserved, no special consideration. There is no doubt that by the mid-1960s there was a fairly strong anti-intellectual feeling among teachers. This gave rise to the growth of the movement for 'gifted children', a movement resented and disliked by many schools.

The arguments from justice joined easily with the Dewey-based principles discussed above. Both led away from competition, and towards a kind of co-operative concept of learning. Many headteachers professed to despise and dislike examinations, describing certificates as 'mere bits of paper', and teaching for specific syllabuses as 'cramming the head with facts'. Some extreme theorists, such as Eric Midwinter, carried such arguments so far that he held it wrong to enter children from deprived backgrounds for any kind of examinations, since they were bound to fail. They should not be introduced to a culture that was alien to them, but instead should be taught and guided through their own 'working-class' culture, in which they could succeed. Thus the desire that no one should fail became, among some educationalists, a means of totally cutting some children off from any possible means of succeeding, in the normal sense of the word. Such excesses, however, were rare. But the conjunction of hostility to competition and hostility to the kind of authoritarianism thought to be implied in 'old-fashioned' teaching was a powerful influence in many comprehensive schools in the late 1960s and 1970s. Motivated partly by political considerations, partly by educational theory only indirectly political in content, teachers and the trainers of teachers rejected absolutely the idea that education should be directed towards any service or economic end. 'Vocational' education was, in their view, a contradiction. Training might be goal-directed, but education must be pure and undertaken for the sake of the 'growth' of the child.

Whether connected logically or only chronologically, while

this, or something like it, was the consensus in maintained schools, in universities there was an equal rejection of authority, here mostly among students themselves. While school education was just beginning to be suspected of extravagance, in the early sixties, paradoxically there was an explosion of growth in university education. Following the Robbins Committee Report in 1963 new universities sprang up all over the country and tertiary education in general was in a state of unexampled euphoria. Alongside the new universities themselves, starting their degree courses from scratch and employing large numbers of sometimes rather dubiously qualified new lecturers, there was a parallel development in the polytechnics, many of them offering degree courses for the first time, and devising courses in subjects such as literature, languages, and philosophy that had nothing whatever to do with the technology-based courses for which they had first been invented. All this local authority-financed expansion was subject to the liberal, though very thorough, validation procedures of the newly invented Council for National Academic Awards (CNAA). The Council was charged with the task of seeing that the new courses were of degree standard, but was powerless to adjudicate on the wisdom or otherwise of there being so many arts-orientated courses in the first place. It seemed in truth a time of indulgent expansion; and, as if in retribution, students of all kinds, in universities old and new and in the polytechnics, became more and more resistant to authority, not just social authority, but the academic authority of their teachers and of the disciplines within which they were studying.

Often the new students could not say what they were rejecting. The accepted principle was that you should not define your cause before starting the revolution. If you were in revolt, a cause would emerge.

As a matter of fact, there was a sense, in the UK, in which much of this revolutionary fervour was second-hand, the disturbances mere copy-cat revolts based on what had happened in Paris in 1968 or in America in subsequent years. It would now be impossible and unprofitable to trace the various events, and their consequences, in all the universities and polytechnics in the country. The details, fortunately, are unimportant. What happened is indisputable: students, and the institutions to which they belonged, acquired a bad name universally. Students came to be regarded as trouble-making drones, supported by the taxpayers' money, indulging themselves at others' expense, and frivolously wasting their own and other people's time. The reputation of the universities and polytechnics has hardly recovered to this day. Historically, the behaviour of the students in the five or so years starting in 1969 can be seen as one more blow to education, one more reason for the public to begin to demand that they should have more control over the educational system.

And so, by 1977, there was pretty widespread dissatisfaction with education in all its forms. The consumers, the pupils, were certainly dissatisfied. At school they were showing their displeasure by truanting in ever-increasing numbers. Those who received them as school-leavers were equally discontent. People straight from school were not competent for employment, or even for further training. This was the allegation. There was muttering too in the universities about a general decline in standards of literacy and numeracy among undergraduates. Parents began to turn in increasing numbers to the independent schools. It was not surprising therefore that while politicians and public demanded change, schools, teacher-training establishments, and educationalists were vaguely and inconclusively defensive about the product that was on offer in State schools.

There was, in particular, deep and widespread dissatisfaction with the mathematical attainments of children at school. Ted Wragg, describing his work as adviser to the Parliamentary Select Committee into the attainment of the school leaver (1976/7), reports that mathematics was the topic that came up by far the most frequently in all the submissions to that Committee, and one of its recommendations was that an inquiry should be set up into mathematics teaching. At first the DES did not accept the need for such an inquiry, but soon the Cockcroft Committee was established, and they published their report under the title *Mathematics Counts*.[4] While this sort of dissatisfaction was being aired, the Manpower Services Commission, established in 1974 as an offshoot of the Department of Trade and Industry, was becoming increasingly important in the training of the young unemployed: the education service seemed more and more to be poor, mean and irrelevant when contrasted with the up-to-date and positively useful service of training.

At the same time, education, which had always in fact been a political matter, if only because of the vast sums of public money spent on it, became increasingly and more obviously political because of the politicization of local government. In the old days before the local government reorganization of 1974, it had been possible for Local Education Authorities to make their decisions relatively autonomously, with a view to the educational needs of local children, and under the guidance of often very high-powered and imaginative Chief Education Officers. This was perhaps especially true of authorities in the counties. For example, in Oxfordshire the statutory Education Committee was mainly composed of old-style landed Tories, but with a mixture of keen Trades Unionist members from Cowley, and some 'intellectuals' deliberately invited in from the university. Guided by the Chief Officer, the county became one of the first to introduce comprehensive schools of a new style, as well as fresh methods of teaching in its primary schools, and an immense explosion of organized music teaching all over the county. Similar stories could be told of West Yorkshire, Leicestershire, and many other counties. The crucial factor in these committees was the presence on them of members and officers together. With reorganization the Education Committees changed in character. Officers were no longer members, and increasingly education came to be seen not as a separate or specialized concern of local government but as a service to be considered alongside housing, transport, or rubbish collection. Partly because of the earlier bitterness of the battle over comprehensive reorganization, more because in the new artificially contrived areas (such as 'Humberside', 'Avon', 'Kirklees', and 'Thamesdown') there was no tradition and no sense of local needs, political alignments became overwhelmingly important. Where a council had a plain political majority, educational decisions were now taken on party lines. There was simply no place for the relatively specialized, politically disinterested decision-making, specific to education, that the old Education Committees had provided. Moreover in 1977 the Association of Education Committees was disbanded. There was no longer any forum where education as an essential, local provision could be discussed, and there was no pressure group to speak for this aspect of national education.

This, then, is the state we are in as we approach the 1990s. I doubt if my picture, though depressing, is too gloomy. There is no consensus about what education should be, what it is for, either in schools or places of higher education. There is widespread ignorance about what does or should go on in schools or universities. The retreat of individuals to the private sector simply obscures the deep troubles of national education as a whole. Schools and universities are told with increasing shrillness that they are failing in their duties, but there is no agreement about what those duties are.

Discontent with the outcome of education carries with it a general low esteem for those who dispense this unsatisfactory commodity, the teachers. School teachers are among the most despised, and also the worst-paid, sectors of society. Understandably, there is a shortage of good people wanting to join the profession; and the strikes of 1985–7 did nothing to improve the status of school teachers in the public esteem. This alone is a factor that enormously complicates any discussion of school education.

How are we to get out of the present mess? This is the question I shall address in the following chapters. I shall try as far as possible to discuss matters of principle rather than of particular detail. But in a time of rapid change it is difficult always to separate the two. By way of background to what follows, I must first state my position on two related issues, since they are issues that may arise over and over again in the discussion of education at the present time.

The first is the issue of comprehensive schools. The Conservative Party did not take up any definite stand on comprehensive schools when it came into office in 1979. As I hope to have suggested, the main educational debate had by then turned from its concentration on the organization of education, characteristic of the 1960s, to the consideration of its content and its costs. The question must arise again now, if only because people have suggested that in order to improve the education of our children we need to move back to some system of selection (see for example *Whose Schools? A Radical Manifesto*, published by the Hillgate Group in 1986). There is an argument of increasing popularity with government and some of the advisers to government, that since comprehensive schools are widely seen to do worse for their pupils than selective schools in terms of examination results, and since so many people, if they can afford it, are removing their children from the maintained comprehensive sector to independent schools (which are broadly speaking selective) a way must be found for government to supply non-comprehensive schools, in the interests of the country as a whole. There are massive holes in this line of argument; but, roughly, the view is that since employers are not getting what they want from comprehensive schools, they are certain to get it, or *more* of it, from selective schools.

There are three conclusions drawn from these arguments, all to some extent encapsulated in the 1988 Education Reform Bill, though it is not altogether clear how the proposals are related to each other.

First, a new kind of selective school is to be established, financed and managed by educational trusts and independent of Local Authorities. The money to set up these trusts is to be supplied by industry, and the schools are to be founded for the most part in inner cities, and are to be technological in character. They will be known as City Technology Colleges, and they will be selective, though how and according to what criteria the pupils are to be chosen is not yet clear. There will be relatively few of such schools. I shall consider them further in Chapter 2. But it is perhaps worth noticing here that firms have not been conspicuously forthcoming with offers to fund the schools, and the DES itself has had to put up considerable sums to support the first of them. Indeed it may be asked why companies whose first duty is to their shareholders should put huge sums into the education system.

Secondly, it has been proposed in some quarters that there

should be a more general return to the old grammar school system (and indeed in a few areas these schools remain). This proposal has been partially absorbed in a different suggestion, that schools may decide for themselves whether or not to dissociate themselves from their Local Authority and become independent, relying on the DES to pay for their pupils by direct grant. Such schools might, gradually, become selective, and indeed might be very like the old direct grant schools, abolished by the Labour Government in 1966. Parents, it is proposed, will determine whether a particular school should opt out of Local Authority control, or should stay in. The question of 'opting out' has been controversial, and doubts have been expressed about the methods proposed for establishing the will of the parents. Moreover it is less than clear from the Bill what advantages are supposed to accrue to a school if it separates itself from a Local Authority, unless doing so is thought in general to be advantageous (where, for instance, a Local Authority is unduly 'political'). Many of the services now provided to schools by the LEA (such as careers advice, or the services of educational psychologists) would have to be 'bought in' by the school. But there is at least a hint in the Bill that in certain circumstances opted-out schools (to be referred to as grant-maintained schools) might receive extra funds from the DES: although in general such schools are to receive funding equivalent to that which they would have received from the LEA, Clause 67 (3) and (4) lay down that for certain 'special purposes' extra non-recurrent or recurrent grants may be forthcoming. Moreover in *The Tablet* (16 April 1988) Shirley Williams pointed out another advantage that grant-maintained schools might have: Mr Baker has laid down that LEA schools must take in children up to the 1979 limit of numbers, so that as many parents as possible can get their children in, if they choose a particular school. But the 1979 limit represented the highest possible number of children for a school—higher than was desirable, since it was imposed in order to deal with the rise in the birth-rate of the mid-1960s. If schools were obliged to take in this maximum number, they might opt out, since as a grant-maintained school their numbers would be fixed not by the 1979 limit, but by the article of government of that particular school. A grant-maintained school could thus become smaller and, automatically, more selective.

The third proposal is that parents should have absolute rights to choose the school that their children should attend. The intention is that 'good' schools, even if comprehensive, will be chosen by parents, 'bad' schools will be left unchosen. Market forces would then bring it about that 'bad' schools would simply wither away, or be compelled to become 'good', if they were to remain open. How such market forces are supposed to work in the field of education is far from clear. But presumably if the 'good' schools became, as a result of their location, their examination results, or by some other means, identifiable in the eyes of parents, then these schools would have to become selective. They could not expand enough to accommodate all who chose them. In that case we should be back in something like the unsatisfactory position we were in before the introduction of comprehensive schools, when the least successful children were relegated to schools that were openly admitted to be inferior; and it is likely that the 'good' schools would, many of them, choose to free themselves from their Local Authorities. So the Local Authorities would be left to administer only those schools that nobody wanted to go to. There could scarcely be a more manifest recipe for disaster.

The basis for all these conclusions seems to be that because there are bad comprehensive schools the system must be abandoned (and if this is not the intention it is likely to be the consequence of present policies). The principle of genuine secondary education for all, which led to the establishment of comprehensive schools in the first place, has, it seems, to be given up in favour of 'good' education for some and 'bad' for others, the 'good' now being variously identified with the rigorous, the vocational, and the wealth-producing. That there is a certain amount of confusion and inconsistency in the arguments does not make them less to be feared. It is, indeed, essential to try to embark on reform from a different base. We ought to argue that since there are undoubtedly some good successful comprehensive schools, we must use these as models for the rest. This is not an argument based on a desire for equality or even for justice. It is an *educational* argument based on what children need, and what we as society need from them. We cannot afford any longer to waste the abilities of 80 per cent of all the children in the maintained system by relegating them to a 'worse' form of education. They need to be educated properly, and society desperately needs them as educated members. The comprehensive system is by far the simplest and most cost-effective way of educating children according to their needs.

It is very important that we recognize the possibility of accepting the best features of comprehensive schools while getting rid of the worst, remembering with reasonable humility that the schools were introduced in the first place as experimental, and that all the trial and error may not yet be over. We should remind ourselves that to accept the comprehensive ideal does not entail extremes of mixed-ability teaching. It does not forbid separating children in sets, according to their abilities and their interests. It does not compel us to embrace the principle of total integration of all handicapped children, including the disruptive, into the ordinary class-room. Within a comprehensive school it is perfectly possible for children to be ambitious and competitive, for them to submit to a proper discipline, one imposed both by their teachers, and by the rigours of the subject itself that they are studying. Teachers in comprehensive schools can be as imaginative and as devoted as in any other kind of school. The comprehensive ideal is simply the ideal that holds *all* children worthy to be educated. It is the ideal of what has been called 'the democratic intellect'; and it is not the intellect alone that we are concerned with, but morality, judgement, and taste. In a culture more and more unified by the mass media, it is more absurd and anachronistic than ever to separate the middle-class from the working-class, the potentially academic and scholarly from the rest, in terms of the teaching they will receive at school. If we want, as we do, an intelligent, open, ambitious population from whom managers and workers alike will be drawn, to say nothing of creative and imaginative people in all fields, then the segregation of children into different schools must be wrong.

It follows that whatever conclusions we may reach about the content of the school curriculum, and however varied and flexible the curriculum itself and the examination of it may be, the curriculum should be essentially designed for comprehensive schools.

It is not practical politics to abolish private schools, nor do I believe it right to do so, in the interests of freedom. But it should be made clear that educational excellence is to be found in the comprehensive schools of the State system, and indeed that these schools should take the lead both in educational experiment and in the democratizing of education as a whole. The most important lesson we can learn from our present educational disarray is that education is for *everybody*. We have got not merely to say this, but to believe it and put our belief into practice. When I write about secondary education, then, in the following pages, I shall have in mind comprehensive schools.

The second general issue is that of local control over maintained secondary schools. The new pattern that will gradually take shape towards the end of this century is of a centrally determined national curriculum, individual schools being given their own budgets to spend as they think fit within the legally required curriculum framework. The DES published a paper early in 1988, entitled *Local Management of Schools*, setting out how this is to work in practice. As we have seen, schools are also to be given the option of leaving the Local Authority altogether and becoming in some sense independent, though with non-fee-paying pupils. This independence, however, has no bearing on the central control of the curriculum, since all maintained secondary schools, whatever their source of funding, will be subject to the same law with regard to the curriculum.

However, the issue of a central curriculum must be separated from that of more general control of the schools, or responsibility for them. The two issues are frequently discussed together, but this tends to lead to confusion. The justification for introducing a national curriculum is to answer the quite general criticism of our schools, that they are not teaching children what they need to know (or what we need them to know). The national curriculum can be seen as the answer, albeit belated, to the demands of the Great Debate. Most politicians, and probably most of the general public, whatever their political party, regard it as in principle a sensible innovation, certainly one that will give parents a better notion of what they ought to expect, in whatever part of the country their children may go to school. In a speech at a North of England conference at the beginning of 1987 Kenneth Baker, the Secretary of State for Education and Science, referred to the eccentricity of the British system of education compared with that of other European countries, all of whom had a national common curriculum. Our system used indeed to be described as 'a national system, locally administered'. But Mr Baker argued that we could not really be said to have a national system at all when there is no nationally agreed curriculum. He said 'we cannot continue with a system under which teachers decide what people should learn without reference to clear nationally agreed objectives, and without having to expose, and if necessary justify, their decisions'. Of course this makes the present situation sound dramatically worse than it is. For the most part, children, whether at primary or at secondary school, learn much the same, wherever they are at school; and the system of public examinations, externally monitored, ensures that there is a reasonable degree of uniformity. Especially in secondary schools, teachers have always been subject to the constraints of this system, based on what their pupils need in the way of qualifications, as well as the more general considerations of what their pupils ought to know. But in the past there was certainly considerable diversity in secondary schools at least about what subjects were compulsory for all pupils, and how soon they might give them up. The national curriculum should do nothing but good if it is a means of ensuring that schools do not, for example, permit children to give up all science subjects at the age of thirteen, or fail to reach a reasonable competence in reading and calculating by the time they leave school. Nor does the familiar bogy of the French Minister of Education, said to know exactly what every child at school is learning that minute, when he looks at his watch, seem so very alarming even if it conformed in any way with the truth. Why not? Even if every child of thirteen was learning algebra at eleven o'clock on a Wednesday, each child would be learning algebra for himself, with the help of his own class teacher. Not all of them would be learning the same thing, parrot-fashion, up and down the country. The problems might be the same, nation-wide, but the method of tackling them would quite certainly be different.

A common national curriculum, then, is to be welcomed, and in itself it poses no threat to the Local Authorities, who have in any case been more concerned with the distribution of resources and the advising of schools on the presentation and delivery of the curriculum than with direct curricular decisions. But there is a different aspect of the new movement towards centralized control over education, aimed towards stripping Local Authorities of their general powers in the provision of education. We have seen already how Local Authority power has changed in the last fifteen years, and how as a part of these changes, the Education Committees have become more and more political. The so-called 'Loony Left', much invoked before the general election of June 1987, was in some places responsible if not for vagaries in the total school curriculum, then at least for the expenditure of scarce resources on teachers, and publications, dealing with subjects dear to their hearts, like racism, sexism, and peace-studies, unpopular with government and with many parents. There must have been a suspicion that under the control of these Authorities only left-wing teachers need apply for jobs, and that money that might have been spent on education was being spent elsewhere; for example, on supporting lesbian or 'gay' groups. The old notion of partnership between central and local government had long disappeared. After the election, therefore, it became more and more obvious that 'Authority-bashing' was part of the new programme. In 1986 George Cooke, once Chief Education Officer of Lincolnshire, wrote a book with Peter Gosden on *Education Committees*. In it he argued that 'Education is a very special public service, with unique needs . . . It cannot, except in a thoroughly perverted form, be a satisfactory instrument for party political indoctrination and it cannot live happily in a situation which subjects it continually to the harsher pressures of party political confrontation.'[5] No doubt this is true, but, as we have seen, such confrontations are just as likely now at local as at central level. If anything, arguments against the politicization of education (making it a 'political football') tell rather in favour of central than of local control. Health provision has long been centralized (though with regional elements). There is no intrinsic reason why education, an equally universal and vital need, should remain in local control. For my part I simply cannot predict what effect, for good or ill, this kind of centralization would have on the education service. I would simply suggest that we should not allow either sentimentality or a genuine concern for retaining decentralized powers in general to distract us from the major, and separate, task of attempting to determine a common policy for all education at all stages in the future.

We know at least that we are to have a common centrally determined curriculum for maintained secondary schools. This will ultimately ensure that, without further intervention, there will also be more uniform provision in the primary schools. For it is within the powers of secondary heads to demand a certain pattern of expectation of children proceeding from primary to secondary education. No one can demand a fixed level of achievement. Children develop at different times and by overcoming different obstacles. This is why it is absurd to lay down specifications as to which books children should have read by the time they are eleven, or what kind of mathematical problems they should be able to solve. And this is why it will be particularly damaging to introduce the tests proposed by the Secretary of State to monitor what children know and can do at fixed ages, 7, 11, and 14. Even with a common core curriculum, there will be enormous and perfectly explicable differences between children's knowledge and abilities at these ages (as anyone who has had more than one child of his own, or has taught a class of children will know). To impose a common curriculum is one thing; to enforce the testing of children in this curriculum at specific ages is quite another. Teaching would thereby be compelled to become rigid and unimaginative, and the possibility of children following their interests at their own pace will be eroded. I shall have more to say about examinations in Chapter 3, but the age-related test proposal is the worst of all proposals. With reasonable flexibility, it is for heads of primary and secondary schools jointly to ensure that children at primary school do not waste their time, and that they continue to advance when they change schools.

A cautionary word should perhaps be entered here. In order not to seem too dictatorial, and perhaps to conform with some grass-roots grocer-Tory image, ministers have sometimes spoken as if their aim was not so much to take powers to themselves (and thus away from Local Authorities) as to give powers to parents. Parents are accorded a totally new status in the 1988 Bill. There is a danger that parents may become the new fashion, the non-political perfect solution to any aggressive problem arising between the local and the national. Lord Joseph (as Secretary of State, Sir Keith) saw to it that there should be more parents on the governing bodies of schools; and since then they have been more and more frequently invoked. They are spoken of as 'the consumers' or 'the customers', those who in the end have to approve the 'product'. There is a false analogy contained in such expressions. Customers or consumers can be expected to judge a product by their own taste or good sense. They know what they want, and, if they pay, they are entitled to have it. Within reason, the more choice they have the better. They are, in practical terms, the experts. Parents, on the contrary, are not experts on educational matters, or most of them are not. Certainly they want their children to do well; they want the best for them. But most of them have no means of knowing how this happy outcome should be brought about. The general public are, on the whole, pretty conservative about education. If they think about it at all, they think of a mythical golden age when children at school were naturally obedient, and, if not, were forced to learn and to remember what they were told. Indeed there is a paradox here. Many of today's parents were themselves at school in the 1960s, the height of the 'horti-cultural' era of education. Yet there is evidence (for example in the numerous letters written to women's magazines on educa-tional matters) that they believe themselves to have spent their school-days sitting at their desks reciting the multiplication tables and learning how to parse sentences in the English language. They write as if totally familiar with raps over the knuckles and old-fashioned dictation. They write in fact as if they were 60, not 30 or 40. I cannot explain this phenomenon: I merely record it. But perhaps this odd time-shift on the part of many parents demonstrates their unsuitability to be the new source of power to determine the future content of the curriculum, or to protect educational standards.

It has to be said that many parents themselves share this view. In Scotland, where parent power in schools is further ahead than in England and Wales, and where parents will have the right to select headteachers or dismiss members of the teaching staff, as well as influencing the general policy of the school, many parents expressed their doubts about adopting such a role when the new school year started in 1987. They were the first to say that they would prefer to trust all this to people who knew something about education.

Parents have another drawback. Most of them are interested in education, if at all, only so long as their own children are at school. There is an inbuilt discontinuity in parent power which may mean that the most influential voices on the governing body suddenly fall silent. Finally, the Secretary of State should not forget that parents do not form a uniform, obedient, like-minded body of consumers. Parents are also political. The most energetic of them may form themselves into pressure-groups of a not wholly child-centred kind. The resulting conflict can be harmful both to schools and to individual pupils. If we did not know this before, we have learned it from the actions of parents in Dewsbury who, at the beginning of the school year 1987/8, refused to allow their children to attend a local primary school that was predominantly Muslim. They took them to a school of their choice some distance away, which could not, according to Local Authority policy, accept them. It was the children in this case who suffered.

I strongly believe that parents should be properly informed about the policies and practices of their schools; that they should have the means regularly to voice their opinions and should indeed be represented on the governing bodies of schools, yet I believe too that there are dangers in allotting them too many constitutional powers. Even less than Local Authorities are they to be relied on for continuity of policy, or an ability to look beyond the day after tomorrow. Yet parent power has, in the recent past, been one of the central proposals of government.

It is time to turn from the past to the future and consider first what centrally regulated changes in the curriculum for schools would help to raise the overall standard of education of children, nation-wide. Thereafter I shall consider the status and the training of the teachers needed by any improved system of school education. Finally I shall consider consequential changes in the polytechnics and universities. For it is not just school education that is under fire at the present time. Universities have hardly ever been held in lower esteem. It is futile to allocate blame for this. But the fact is that, unless the present lack of respect for the universities of the country can be remedied, education as a whole will not be respected; and if it is *not* respected, then it will not improve. It is of no use to put forward a partial plan for the revitalization of our education. Any plan must cover the whole field. Educationalists and teachers, as well as members of the Government, must come to think of schools, polytechnics, and universities as engaged in a common enterprise. For this a common policy is required.

Secondary school: the structure of the curriculum

2

In a book concerned with the need for a common policy to cover the education of all children at all stages of their careers, it might be thought right to start with a discussion of the primary school. I shall not do this for two related reasons. First, there seems at present less to complain about in most of our primary schools than in secondary or tertiary education. Neither parents nor politicians are crying out for radical reform of the system. There are obviously improvements to be made; more science should be taught, and there is a great need for more specialists in the class-room, even if they have to be peripatetic teachers, shared between a number of schools. Only so will children be sure to get a proper grounding in science, mathematics and music; only so will children with special educational needs be identified and given the help they must have. But such reforms are not radical.

Secondly, any changes that come to the primary schools must come as a result of changes at the secondary level. It is essential that the two stages should be coherent. In the 1960s there was felt to be a vast gap not only between those primary schools where the teaching was 'traditional' and those where it was 'advanced' or 'child-centred', but also between primary and secondary schools. The aims of the two sectors sometimes appeared, both to parents and children, to be quite different. At present all the pressure for reform is on the secondary schools, and this because of the new wave of vocationalism that has swept over education since the late 1970s. Secondary school is, after all, nearer to life after school, and it is about this that schools are increasingly urged to think. Whatever national curriculum we have at secondary school, this curriculum will have consequences for primary school. Just as in the private sector primary education is 'preparatory', getting children ready for their public schools, so in the maintained sector we may naturally see primary school in this light. It is not that primary teachers must become preoccupied with examinations or tests to be taken at the time when a child changes school. It is rather that the whole point of a national curriculum will be lost if it cannot be assumed that children at 11 will be ready for whatever is the generally agreed content of the first year at secondary school.

Such interconnection between the two sectors, primary and secondary, should not be thought of as a burden. As more graduates enter primary teaching, so I believe it will become easier for schools to have a common purpose and to recognize this in a jointly worked-out curriculum, with more communication and actual cross-over from one part of the system to the other. It is therefore unnecessary to discuss primary education separately.

At the secondary level we are certainly in for a decade of reform. Now is the time when we must be absolutely convinced that we are getting things right. A national curriculum centrally determined is about to be imposed on the schools, and this is bound to encapsulate a philosophy of education, its nature and purpose, that arises directly out of the discontents of the last twenty years. For it is in secondary education, and in the transition from secondary education to the next stage, that we are being asked to admit the failure of the system, whether this is measured by parental dissatisfaction or by the number of school and university leavers who do not satisfy their potential employers.

Even extremists of the 1960s, who believed that the task of a school was to ensure that children enjoyed themselves while they were pupils, must have had in mind, as well, *some* further outcome, some advantage that would flow in the long run to the children who had been encouraged, under that regime, to 'grow' and 'blossom' and 'flourish' in the 'learning situation' provided by the class-room. The 'flourishing' was not meant to end when the school door closed. For no one concerned with education could deny that, in teaching, teachers are looking to the future of the child. The future may be seen narrowly in terms of what will happen to the children when they move out of this class, or this school, to the next stage; but ultimately whether or not they have been properly educated will be judged in terms of what happens to them later, when they have left school. This is how teachers will think. Those who are not teachers, whether they are concerned with the good of society or with the good of certain individual children, will even more certainly look to what happens after school if they are to be satisfied with what goes on in school itself. In what way will children be better off for having been to school than they would be if they had stayed at home? How will other members of society benefit from having expensively financed their being there? These are the questions to be answered. We, society as a whole, must decide what we want school to do; and if we cannot agree on this we are not entitled to complain that schools, and teachers, fail to give us what we want, nor can we hope to find ways to improve the situation.

If we could agree on what we want, whether for our children or for society, the task of government would be relatively straightforward. Parliament could, either directly or through the Local Authorities, implement what the public as a whole demanded. But in spite of a pretty widespread discontent with education as it is, there is no clear view of what it should be. There is probably an equal number of people, for example, who think that the less able have a poor deal, and that the system should be geared more towards improving their lot, and on the other hand of those who think that it is the most able who suffer, and that we are wasting our educational resources unless we tilt the system towards them. In the absence of consensus, government has to be bold enough to propose its own answers, and these must be seen to incorporate an underlying principle, carried through and exemplified in all of the stages of education from primary to tertiary. Piecemeal solutions are not enough in education, and it is time we recognized this. Such is the burden of what I hope to argue in the next chapters.

This sounds of course like rampant centralization. And it may be argued that centralist solutions are dangerous, not only because in any particular administration they may be used to bad effect, but because in principle they inhibit freedom. Now it is true that if any government tried to lay down exactly what should be taught in universities and polytechnics there would be a great outcry, quite properly. Academic freedom in higher education is something we prize highly. We are familiar with the spectacle of its loss, in pre-war Germany, for example, and in present-day Russia and China; and so we are the more determined to preserve it for ourselves. I shall have more to say about this in Chapter 5. But such arguments are not applied to what is taught at school, though if we were sincere followers of J. S. Mill we should apply them. He argued in his essay *On Liberty* that State schools, with a State control over the curriculum, would be simply a means of producing a docile and *bien pensant* population, moulded in accordance with the wishes of the government of the day. However, despite some lip-service to the rights of schools to determine their own curriculum, on the whole those who argue against centralist control of schools do so not so much on grounds of loss of freedom for schools as on grounds of the consequent loss of local power.

This reflects an extremely important difference between schools and universities. Schools are not, and can never be, autonomous. Whatever the role of teachers, it is not to push back the frontiers of knowledge, nor to determine a new direction in which a discipline can move. Despite the possibility of infinite variation in detail and in method, those who teach in school have to admit that realistically they will teach broadly what is required, either by employers or by the universities themselves. If only because school is for *everyone*, because it is compulsory, both government and the public have a right that they do not have in universities to take part in the determination of the curriculum. But since the universities also have a central part to play in this determination, co-operation between Government and universities is of the greatest importance. The principles that run through the total education system have to be agreed between them.

Since 1977, for reasons suggested in the last chapter, there has been considerable concern among both politicians and the public with the utility of education to society. What do *we* need from children when they leave school, college, or university? What will be of the greatest use in our attempts to improve economic growth and output? Such questions are, of course, perfectly legitimate, and indeed necessary for any government prepared to expend large sums of public money on education. Yet it is damaging to suggest that they can be answered separately from questions about the educational needs of children and young people themselves. To attempt such a separation tends to lend colour to a distinction often drawn within the curriculum at school or within the range of subjects studied in higher education between the useful and the useless. This in turn tends more and more to be seen as a division between science subjects (useful) and arts subjects (useless).

For example, in the 1985 Green Paper on the future of the universities (altogether a somewhat hasty and ill-expressed document) it was suggested that more money should be given to universities, and more places offered to students, for sciences than for the arts, and this policy is now being implemented, with considerable effect on the schools. When the universities reacted unfavourably to this aspect of the paper, accusing its authors of philistinism, the then Secretary of State, Sir Keith Joseph, was quick to reply that he was not against the arts subjects: far from it. He recognized that they were 'enriching' for the school students and undergraduates who studied them. Thus immediately he managed to drive a wedge between the virtuous students, worthy of support, who studied sciences for the sake of society, and the self-indulgent arts students who pursued their chosen subject for the sake of their own benefit.

There are two things wrong with such a suggested division. In the first place it is necessary to recognize the identity that exists between the interests of students (whether at school or in places of higher education) and of society. Students *are* society, or society in the making. A benefit to them is a benefit to society, and a body of students personally 'enriched' by their education is an 'enriched' society. No education worth the name is wholly self-regarding, nor on the other hand can any be treated as wholly instrumental or other-regarding.

Secondly, and far more important, the distinction implicitly made by Sir Keith is misleading with regard to the nature of the distinction between arts and sciences. In the presumption that the study of science and mathematics is 'useful' there is latent a new and harmful kind of philistinism, based partly on ignorance. For instance, many people assume that a student engaged in the study of engineering at university will be able to make things and mend them. After all, the word 'engineer' used to be used for the person who could drive and maintain a car, in the early days of motoring. It is still instinctively held that those involved in engineering science should be useful handymen and will have oil on their hands. In fact, engineering science is, or may be, an extremely abstract and theoretical science. Again, mathematicians are notoriously not all competent accountants; physicists may not be interested in or fitted for involvement in industrial processes—they may not even be able to change a light bulb. Research in any of the sciences, including medicine, may be totally 'unproductive'; it may have no immediate bearing on making, mending, or curing. Its aim may be the advancement of knowledge and understanding, without obvious practical implications. To forget the existence of pure science and mathematics and pure research in these disciplines is to misunderstand the nature of knowledge itself, and would be just as much a corruption of the idea of education and learning as would neglect of philosophy and other arts subjects. Philistinism can show in more ways than one. It is not only those who dismiss the arts as self-indulgent who lay themselves open to such a charge. And so it is necessary to ask how we are to transform the distinction commonly drawn between arts and sciences, or perhaps replace it, deep though it goes in the structure of our educational curriculum.

It was powerfully argued by Bernard Williams, in his Raymond Priestley Lecture delivered in Birmingham in 1986, that to study the humanities is as useful as to study the sciences. It is not enough, he argued, to defend the study of the arts in school or university on the ground that it is a vaguely civilizing luxury, agreeable for some people to have (like, he suggests, a leather blotter from Harrods). On the contrary, the study of the humanities is essential to society as a whole, since 'the humanities are concerned with a truthful understanding of where we are and where we come from'. Society itself and those who govern it need such understanding; and in a democratic society this entails that the study of the humanities be widely spread, not confined to an élite of self-indulgers, the leather blotter-owning classes.

To argue as Bernard Williams does is to suggest that there is no sharp line to be drawn between the arts and the social sciences; for it is the acknowledged role of the latter to contribute to our understanding of ourselves and our society. Pragmatically this is right. Who is to say with any show of reason whether to place history or, say, political philosophy in one category or the other? But the impossibility of drawing this distinction may be bad for the arts. If the arts are ultimately indistinguishable from the social sciences then they are tainted, tarred with the same unpopular brush. For the concept of the social sciences has provoked extreme, and sometimes ludicrous, reactions in recent years. Keith Joseph, for example, will be remembered at least partly for his violent hostility to the social sciences, even causing the then Social Science Research Council to change its name in the early 1980s to the misleading Economic and Social Research Council. His view of a science was twofold: first, its propositions should be conclusively refutable, and therefore capable of being asserted as facts until such time as they are refuted; secondly, it should be useful. The social sciences could not satisfy either of these criteria. Their propositions were often vague and irrefutable by concrete evidence; and though economics and sociology in their early days made great promises for the reform of society through understanding, these promises have not, Sir Keith believed, been fulfilled. No reforms of society have been delivered.

According to Keith Joseph, then, the word 'science' is misused in connection with studies of society itself, and his view is widely shared. I think it is unwise, therefore, to defend arts subjects on the grounds that they are a kind of social science. Moreover in many cases it is implausible. It is hard to see how a minute understanding of the development of the Greek language from Homer to Demosthenes, or of the keys used by Brahms in the second subjects of the first movements of his sonatas can be fitted into the usual pattern of socially useful knowledge. Yet I would wish to argue that such understanding should be encouraged and supported.

Rather than defend the arts on the grounds that they are a branch of the sciences and therefore useful, I believe we should try to start again, attempting to lay on one side both the crude criterion of utility and the assumed category distinction between science and arts, itself in fact equally crude.

According to the Greek view of education, especially the view associated with Plato, the only study that was honourable and respectable was that of mathematics or other equally pure and abstract subjects, such as the theory of harmony and astronomy, or philosophy. The intelligence, by which alone such subjects were supposed to be understood, was thought to be wholly distinct from other, lower, faculties. These lower faculties were employed in practical activities, the performance of which was to be relegated, as far as possible, to lower kinds of people, not worthy to be fully educated. Such people were held to be possessed of none of the attributes of pure intellect, the cultivation of which was the purpose of education.

The superiority of the abstract over the concrete, the theoretical over the practical, was taken for granted by the Greeks, and also by all education based on the classical model. It is an assumption that has had a profound and, it is now seen, a damaging effect on schools. But to perpetuate a division between arts and sciences, the useless and the useful, is in my view just as damaging. The dichotomy is different, the line drawn in a different place from where Plato drew it, but the harm to education is just as great. If we genuinely believe everyone to be entitled to education, then we must reject the aristocratic distinction between an education fit only for workers and one fit for philosopher-kings; but we must equally reject the new assumption that only those who are receiving a scientific education are being 'properly' educated; the rest, those who are studying arts, being relegated to the position of drones or parasites to be, at best, tolerated, and seen as 'enriching' themselves. There must be a unifying goal for education, cutting across the old Platonic distinction between the theoretical, or intellectual, and the practical, and *also* across the newly emphasized distinction between technology and science on the one hand and 'arts' on the other.

Of course there is no possible d⋯ ⋯ur need for people so educated that they may fill the ⋯ ⋯ at present unfilled, or offered to people from ⋯ ⋯ because of our own shortage of skilled and ⋯ ⋯ This is perhaps the most urgent dem⋯ ⋯ ⋯s of further education; it is c⋯ ⋯ ⋯ ⋯cause for complaint ag⋯ ⋯

But the⋯ are dange⋯ ⋯ ⋯ ⋯n such compl⋯ ⋯ which nee⋯ ⋯ ⋯ ⋯bout a sho⋯ ⋯ of people who kno⋯ ⋯ to operate ⋯ ⋯ctronic eq⋯pment and car⋯ ⋯ new ⋯ ⋯ ⋯ ⋯about a ⋯hortage of people ⋯ho will invent such ⋯ ⋯Are we complaining that p⋯ ⋯ ⋯ ⋯ ⋯versity unvers⋯ in computer ⋯ ⋯ or unable ⋯ ⋯ ⋯puter? The fact ⋯s that we n⋯ ⋯ ⋯th, and the two ⋯ ⋯ ⋯e confused. We ⋯also need p⋯ ⋯who wil⋯ ⋯ ⋯ ⋯agers, teachers, jo⋯nalists, ⋯ ⋯ ⋯ ⋯ ⋯ with general practica⋯ ability, cer⋯ ⋯ but with more than this. If universal educatio⋯ is a genuine ideal; if, unlike the Greeks, we may claim to believe in such a thing as a democratic intellect, then we must stop thinking of a kind of people, a 'work-force' who will obediently slot into the place society has for them, trained as a kind of technological army. But equally we must stop thinking of another kind of people, ignorant of technology, and interested only in high culture.

In the early 1970s, in the heyday of abstract philosophy of education, it was commonplace to draw a distinction between education 'in the true sense' and pseudo-education; or, which came to the same thing, between education and training. For instance, Michael Oakeshott, in his essay 'Education: the Engagement and its Frustrations', maintained that true education was essentially unconcerned with anything outside itself: 'It is an intrinsic good. If anyone is educated with a goal in mind, to be a doctor, a lawyer or a computer programmer, then what this person is experiencing, whatever he, or his teachers, may think, is not education, but something else.'[1] Similarly, in the same year, John Wilson wrote: 'So long as we are concerned to turn out pupils who are good middle-class boys or skilled technicians [then we are not really concerned with education but with training]. For whereas we can train . . . pupils for particular roles and performances, what we have to educate is people.'[2] Whatever we are supposed to understand by a 'person' we are to believe that educating him will not be directly related to the roles and tasks he has to perform after his education is over. Quite apart from the emotive language of 'turning out' (and related expressions, beloved of Wilson, such as 'fodder for industry'), the whole tone of these remarks seems extraordinarily remote from the way we are accustomed to think today. We are no longer in the least likely to adopt such a Plato-like attitude towards the needs of industry or the economy. Unemployment and economic collapse have changed our views.

Nevertheless, we must not be so swiftly carried away by talk of the job-market as to forget our democratic belief in the value of education as a good in itself, for everyone; nor our individualistic belief in the concept of educational need. Both of these ideals have after all been incorporated in legislation, the first in the 1944 Education Act, the second in that of 1981. The Michael Oakeshott/John Wilson view of education is almost purely Platonic. Those who receive training are lesser than those who receive education. Education is for philosopher-kings. It is something at last to have left such views behind. But we must beware of going too far the other way.

So how are we to reach any agreement now, at the end of the 1980s, on the function of education, what it is for, what needs it must meet?

Broadly, we must agree that in so far as education is failing, it is in its failure to provide some children, too many, with the means to lead a satisfactory life when they leave school. But we have to recognize that the ingredients of a satisfactory life are numerous. And since children are already members of society the nature of their lives, and especially their lives as they grow up and leave school, is a part of the nature of society. The good for them and the good for society cannot be separately assessed. The economic strength of society is not something that can be peeled off and thought of separately from the quality of the life of those who are members of that society.

In James Callaghan's famous speech at Ruskin College, Oxford, in October 1976, from which the Great Debate emerged, he spoke of a school curriculum which would aim 'to equip children . . . for a lively, constructive place in society, and also fit them for a job of work'. Unexceptionable words, perhaps, and certainly non-élitist; not a bit like Plato. But they seem to carry the implication that society exists as a fixed structure, with slots into which school-leavers (or university-leavers) must be fitted. And there was more than a hint, throughout the speech, that education was *primarily* instrumental, not a good in itself. What should be remembered is that there exist many things which are *both* good in themselves *and* good as an instrument or a means to something else. Among such things might be numbered health, food, love, marriage, and, I suggest, education itself.

Obviously getting work is an extremely important goal for any child at school, and it is a goal for society that there should be as low a level of unemployment as is compatible with the advancement of technology and the efficiency of industry and agriculture. But it is not enough to talk about 'jobs' as if, provided enough people have jobs, all is well. For not all jobs are interesting or satisfying. And though most people hold that working in any kind of job is better than not working, it is equally important, and not just for individuals but for society as a whole, that children should be educated so that they can find satisfaction outside their work as well as within it, in things other than paid work. I do not mean to distinguish here between 'work' and 'leisure'; nor am I arguing, on the basis of such a distinction, that 'education for leisure' is just as important as 'education for work', a thesis often defended by those anxious to justify education in sports or indeed in the arts. There may be truth in such a suggestion; and my own dislike of it may stem from nothing more profound than my intense dislike of the word 'leisure', suggesting to me, as it does, the spectacle of some drone-figure sitting in a deck-chair while someone else mows the lawn, or a grim marina, packed with empty yachts. But what truth there is in the suggestion can be put in another and less misleading way. A child at school must certainly be taught those skills which will enable him plausibly to seek and subsequently to hold down a job. But, besides this, he needs a critical awareness of his own world. This entails an awareness of the mutability of this world, and an awareness of what elements in it are permanently to be valued.

We are all prone, especially when we are children, to assume that things have always been as we find them, and that they will never change. One of the major functions of education must be to open people's eyes to the fact that things were at one time different; that they have evolved to where they are now; and that they need not necessarily always remain as they are. We are committed, morally and politically, to treating everyone as free, with a right to see things from his own standpoint and make his own decisions. We are therefore committed to educating everyone so that this freedom is a reality. We must teach children that they can, if they choose, foresee a future different from the past and different from the present; and that they can, if they choose, work towards effecting the changes they foresee.

It is the nature and function of imagination to envisage what is not yet, or is no longer, the case. The democratic ideal, the ideal of free individuals, equally worthy to be educated, depends on the existence of this imaginative faculty in each individual. I would therefore argue that one of the chief tasks of education, perhaps its overriding task, is the education and encouragement of a child's imagination, so that he may not be a slave to a perception confined solely to the present, a perception that is little more than blindness. The teaching of history is one part of such an education; the encouragement of creativity is another, and there are others still.

After primary school, the encouragement of the imagination in children, and the cultivation of specifically creative activities, has often been thought an optional part of the curriculum, a luxury that may have to be dispensed with, left in, if at all, for the less able pupils deemed incapable of serious learning or for that minority determined to reject 'scientific' understanding. Imagination has been associated especially with the arts, and thus in recent years has been increasingly downgraded. This view depends on a radical misunderstanding of the nature of the imagination. Of course we may say of someone that he is imaginative if he is original and spontaneous, and if his work is expressive. But these are not the only signs of imagination. More even than in the free invention of fantasies, or the creation of fictions, the imagination is exercised on the actual and the existent. It is exercised in perception, and the recognition that there is more in what is seen than may meet the casual eye.

Children or adolescents who become absorbed by a particular topic, a specific branch of science or period of history, are exercising their imagination. They see the infinite possibilities in the subject-matter, just as a young child, pretending that the table is a house, sees the possibilities *in* the table, or as the religious person sees and feels God *in* the thunder or the mountainous waves. In the Victorian story, *Eyes and No-Eyes*, we were told of the difference between the characters. Eyes, who saw everything around him as exciting and interesting, was the imaginative one; No-Eyes, bored and truculent, saw the very same things but saw them as boring and limited.

The identification of imagination, not with enhanced perception but with self-expression and 'originality', has had a harmful effect on education. 'Creative' writing has acquired a bad name; it has been contrasted with proper grammatical writing, and has come to be numbered among the suspect activities of the Loony Left, or at least with the 'soft' brigade. And part of the demand for a centralized curriculum, dictated from above, has stemmed from the confused notion that such a curriculum would be not only vocational and future-directed, but strict, narrow, and exact, containing within itself its own criteria of rightness and wrongness. Obviously there is no necessary connection between a common curriculum, imposed centrally, and such rigorousness. A government could, in principle, impose a course of study, the whole aim of which was self-expression. But because the demand for central control has arisen out of a general dissatisfaction with education, and this dissatisfaction is often directed towards an excess of 'creativity' in the classroom, a lack of a disciplined work-force, it is generally assumed that the central common curriculum to be nationally accepted would be down-to-earth, factual, able to be assessed, and marked by a tick or a cross. The demand for central direction, then, partly as we have seen, a demand that the Local Education Authorities should be kept in their place, has become also a demand for a particular *style* of rigorous, and rigorously examined, curriculum. This is often described in the context of 'standards'. High standards in education are equated with low imagination-content. Good, hard, examinable subjects are thought to constitute good education.

It is high time that the concept of imagination was separated from that of the loose, the soft, the non-examinable, and the 'standardless'. An imaginative human being is not a feeble dreamer. He may just as well be a decision-maker, one who can foresee what decisions he will have to make, and what may happen as a result of them. Such a revolution in the perceived role of the imagination, a faculty not peculiar to 'arts' subjects but common to all, is central to educational reform, and is, indeed, the most urgently needed change.

We have to ask by what means this free and forward-looking imagination can be cultivated at school. Perhaps the first essential will sound trivial. Whatever happens to them at school, children must not be bored. Of course they will inevitably suffer moments, even hours, of boredom. But they must not be allowed to become bored with the *whole thing*. They must, all of them, have something to look forward to at school. The superiority of primary over secondary school education lies mainly in the fact that most children of primary school age are open to teaching, and ready to be interested. This has little to do with methods of teaching, or with the curriculum. It has almost everything to do with the age of the child, his ability to become absorbed in a task (whether or not he can see the point of it), and his comparative insulation from the world. As he grows older he is naturally nearer to the world outside school; he is ready to demand a good reason for doing whatever he is asked to do; and he is extremely easily distracted by the problems and dramas of his own life and hard times. Even if we wanted to, we could not make secondary school like

primary school. That is not a possible way to combat boredom.

Yet boredom is the enemy of learning, and the arch-enemy of
long-term educational success. It is also the death of the imagination. But we have to be careful to try to understand what steps are
proper in order to keep it at bay. It is often said that people are
bored at school, and cannot do well, because of the irrelevance of
the curriculum to their own life and experience, or the life and
experience they will have when they leave school. There is truth in
this proposition; but as it stands it is vague and ambiguous. There
are various distinctions that need to be drawn.

There is one sense of 'relevant' in which it means much the
same as 'familiar'. It has sometimes been suggested that there
are groups of children, children of ethnic minorities, for example, or children who are extremely socially deprived, who fail
at school, who play truant and give up all attempt to succeed,
because the content of the curriculum is totally alien to them,
unfamiliar, and therefore irrelevant in a strong sense. To satisfy
such children, it was suggested, nothing but the local and
familiar must be introduced into their curriculum. The aim must
be, in Eric Midwinter's words, 'to familiarize a child with his
environment, in all its moods and manners'.[3]

This is a concept of 'relevance' that must be rejected. For
though it might be claimed that such an education would help
a child to see more in his immediate environment, and understand it better, yet it would also greatly diminish his chances of
going beyond that environment. Equality is not itself a curriculum aim; yet no curriculum that actually sets limits to a child's
future can be acceptable. Education is valued, and has always
been valued, for its liberating effects. It should aim to free a
child from the chains of his environment. He is not committed,
by his education, to rejecting or despising the community in
which he was brought up; but he should be given the means in
some sense to detach himself from it. Only so can he choose
whether to stay in it or leave, only so can he ever see it clearly
enough to try to change it. Only so, furthermore, will he have
the ability to compete with his contemporaries in what is a
world-wide competition. It is of no use to bemoan the existence

of such competition. Derogatory expressions like 'the rat-race' or 'the glittering prizes' do not alter the facts. There could not be devised a sophisticated society in which there was no competition for 'jobs at the top'. It is permanently divisive, as well as educationally mean and unadventurous, to establish deliberately a kind of school within which the curriculum is so inward-looking that those who followed it could not, for example, hope to proceed to higher education or ultimately into one of the professions. Such 'relevance' as this must be rejected, then, on the grounds that it is unjust. It may be rejected also on the grounds that it is patronizing.

This is a danger, as well, for many less extreme forms of 'relevance'. Any teacher who tries to devise a syllabus for a music class that will appeal to the members of the class for its relevance, or who attempts to attract the English class by giving them things to read or act that will speak to them in their own language is in danger of falling into the trap of 'thinking down' to his pupils, of condescending to them.

There is an extraordinarily difficult line to draw here. On the one hand, a school curriculum must fulfil its primary function of serving to open to new ideas the minds of those who follow it. It must introduce new concepts, whether in mathematics, geography, physics or literature, concepts that are unfamiliar, and would have remained unknown to a child who had not been to school. On the other hand these concepts must be introduced in a manner that will make them intelligible. No one can live by abstraction alone. So the abstract must be made concrete by examples. No one can live on a diet of culture that is completely alien. And so, by means of analogies and comparisons, the foreign can be understood in the context of the homely and the familiar. A good teacher will constantly exercise his ingenuity in making the new intelligible. He will never lose sight of who his pupils are, what they can and cannot be expected to take for granted. This is precisely what teaching consists in; and the task will differ according to the age, nationality, and home-background of the pupils. It is a very rare pupil, whether at school or university, who will not understand more with the help of examples and analogies than without, and especially if the examples are simple, intelligible, new, and, if possible, funny.

But throughout all this teaching, this familiarizing and making intelligible, the teacher has to preserve a certain distance. There is, and must remain, a gulf between home and school which must not be eliminated, though it must be crossed by bridges at various points. Shouting across a culture-gap sounds bad. But if school does not retain some ability to perform this apparently fruitless activity, it will in fact have lost its purpose. A child who speaks at home with a powerful local accent, in dialect, with a swear word between every two or three ordinary words, or who hardly speaks English at all, must learn 'proper' talk at school. He must, if necessary (and many children manage this), become bilingual, able to switch as the occasion demands between what may be virtually or actually two languages. If he fails to pick up at school the preferred 'school' language, school will have failed him. And this may be generalized, or taken as some kind of parable. It has application to all areas of the curriculum, and must be borne in mind by curriculum designers. Even if the bottom rung of the ladder is within easy reach of the child, as it should be, the curriculum *is* a ladder. It must reach up beyond the walls of that particular yard within which a child is brought up. It is useless if it does not. 'Relevance' therefore has to be respected, but with caution. It can be no more than the crutch on which the imagination, and freedom, are supported.

The question whether the curriculum is relevant or not is often posed in terms of what a child may need to know, when he leaves the protective environment of school. Pupils themselves, as well as their parents, may ask, 'What's the good of x?' 'What's the good of all that algebra and geometry? I'll never need it.' 'What's the good of your endless French lessons when you can't speak a word of the language at the end of them?' This way of putting the question reveals a sound judgement of the school curriculum: it has to be related to a child's needs, and justified if and only if it satisfies those needs. But we have to remember that human needs are diverse. A human being needs to be able to make himself understood not only when he is shopping or buying a railway ticket, but also when he is expressing his feelings, explaining a principle (of morals or mechanics), or when he is arguing about politics. He must be offered more than the bare minimum. A criterion of *instant* and *obvious* utility cannot be the sole criterion for the inclusion of items in the school curriculum.

•. However, the very persistence of the demand for relevance and usefulness, the dissatisfaction with whatever is seen as 'useless', should lead, as I have suggested, to a more fundamental distinction, not between the useful and the useless, the relevant and the irrelevant, nor between the arts and the sciences, but between the *practical* and the *theoretical*. This distinction, which cuts right across the familiar division into arts and sciences, seems to me by far the most important that there is. This is the dichotomy that must be used to form a framework within which any curriculum change must be placed. If we are to have a national common curriculum, a balance between its practical and theoretical elements must be aimed at, and the balance observed equally in *all* areas of learning.

Plato's ideal education, as we have seen, was founded precisely on such a distinction between the theoretical and the practical, between true knowledge and mere skills. But in Plato's view knowledge was paramount, skills necessarily inferior and suitable only for the lowly. Though I advocate a return to the distinction, as the foundation of education, I am far from endorsing the Platonic evaluation. Indeed, to change this evaluation and thus leave Plato behind is the most important change we have to bring about. The concrete, practical, and technological must be given as much weight and as much prestige as the abstract and theoretical.

What we must change is the hierarchical nature of education. We are too much a prey to the belief that if one kind of education is good, another must be bad, or at least worse than the good. I do not deny, of course, that some schools are better than others, some universities better, others worse. Such comparisons are always possible, and ought to be made, if the worse are to improve. What is wrong, however, is the comparison which places universities at the top because they are thought to be concerned with the abstract and academic, polytechnics below, because of their more technological emphasis (which is itself, as often as not, a myth), and which deems schools to be worth considering only if they are seen as primarily devoted to academic 'standards', imposed from above by the universities themselves. To try to eliminate this way of thinking is difficult; but we must begin. We have to recognize that education must satisfy the needs of its pupils (a highly un-Platonic idea), and that in the case of some children, not necessarily the least able, their needs will be best met by allowing the balance to tip in the direction of the practical. Moreover no child should leave school without some practical competence that can actually be put to use, since we all have practical as well as intellectual needs.

At the time of the 1944 Act, the distinction between the practical and the theoretical was clearly enough recognized. But because of the history of secondary education as clerkly and classical, suitable for future members of the 'learned professions', the division was encapsulated in the division between three, and then two, types of school. In the grammar schools, the practical always took second place. In the secondary modern schools, though in principle it was pursued as a primary goal, as it was in the few technical schools that survived, yet because of the increasing aspiration within the schools themselves that their pupils should be seen to do as well as grammar school pupils, the practical gradually came to be despised there as well. Increasingly candidates thought able enough were entered for O and even A levels (and rightly, because there was at first no other examination for them to take) and when the CSE examination was introduced for those thought not to be up to O level, the top grade of CSE was soon deemed to count as an O level, and thus itself to aspire to the academic. And thus the practical was gradually and increasingly held to be what the 'no-hopers' engaged in. The parity of esteem, demanded in 1944 between the different schools, was never achieved, and could not have been achieved, given the fundamentally Platonic attitude of politicians, teachers, and the general public, to say nothing of the universities.

When comprehensive schools became the norm there was still no serious attempt to rethink the curriculum or the values incorporated within it. Everyone was to be educated on the same campus. But those to be educated were still divided into the sheep and the goats, the most goatish of all doing no examinations before they left school, the best of the sheep doing examinations in none but theoretical or language-based subjects. Attempts to mitigate what were recognized as disastrous divisions often took the form of a refusal to acknowledge the wide difference of ability that existed between pupils, which led to a style and content of teaching roughly directed to the middle band of children, the least and the most able being left to shift for themselves. No radical reform was undertaken of what should be taught, or how what was taught should be valued. In saying this, I do not overlook the enormous amount of on the whole useful and imaginative work on a new-style curriculum undertaken by the Schools Council. But taking up their suggestions and using their materials was always optional; and they had little power to change the general attitude of the public towards the 'non-academic'.

The goats from comprehensive schools, if they were lucky, eventually escaped to be *trained*. In training, at last, the practical came into its own. But the sheep were never trained at all. They were only educated.

The distinction between education and training became increasingly confused and potentially damaging in the early 1980s. Though the demand from industry and society at large was for better school education, the response came at first not from schools but from Youth Training Schemes for school-leavers, organized by the Manpower Services Commission. The Manpower Services Commission was itself dissolved in 1988 and was replaced by a body which took over most of its functions, called the Training Commission. In 1981 there was a government White Paper entitled *New Training Initiatives* which set out the aims of these schemes: to develop skill-training, to provide further education or work-related training for everyone up to the age of 18, and to offer adults the chance to update their skills. Less than a year later the Technical Vocational Education Initiative (TVEI) was announced, and this, though still organized by the MSC, was a scheme that started with pupils at school, in the last two years before their compulsory attendance at school came to an end, and continued until they were 18. The last two years consisted either of a course in the sixth form aimed at technology-related A levels, or with Youth Opportunity training schemes. Many schools chose to enter the scheme as a way of getting fresh resources. But who now was being trained, and who educated? Who was responsible for the curriculum? In 1986 TVEI ceased to be experimental, and in the White Paper *Working Together: Education and Training* the Government put forward the plan for a national scheme with the aim that 'all young people in schools should have the opportunity of following a more relevant and practical curriculum leading to the achievement of recognized standards of competence and qualifications'.

In the light of this kind of development it is high time to drop the distinction between 'education' and 'training' and to refuse to use these words as part of our educational vocabulary. They are, in any case, based on a number of unproved assumptions about how people learn, about the instilling of habits as against the development of understanding which, if they were examined, would probably be found to have no foundation or utility.

In a country in which education up to the age of 16 has become universal and compulsory, and education up to the age of 19 an option for everyone, we have to recognize that this education must be designed to meet pupils' needs. We all of us have needs that are practical as well as those that are to a greater or lesser degree intellectual or theoretical. The consequence of this for the curriculum must be that within all subject areas *both* aspects must be attended to. In every subject, scientific and non-scientific alike, there are two possible approaches, the practical and the theoretical.

The practical is technology-based, at least in the etymologically correct sense of 'skill-based'. Technology itself may be up-to-date, chip-bound, computer-orientated; or it may be simple, and concerned with skills of a less modern kind (though they may be just as difficult to acquire). Technology itself, and its effective use, is not to be confined to the traditional science subjects. Moreover, a thorough understanding of the uses of technology may demand more or less understanding of theoretical science. One may, after all, competently drive a car without understanding much about the principles of the internal combustion engine; one may use a typewriter or a word-processor without being able to make or mend one; one may quickly be taught to use a computer, and make simple programs without being a master of, or even a beginner in, computer science.

The classing together of 'science and technology' has done enormous harm to our educational system, and it has taken place because of a confusion between using tools and techniques of various kinds, and understanding the theory that lies behind them. Learning to use the tools was what, in the past, was called 'training'. But in fact every creative and inventive and imaginative activity (including that of inventing new tools) is better done with the help of 'technology', and so a failure to familiarize children at school with the use of such technology inhibits their imaginative potential, as well as making them incompetent and virtually unemployable when they leave school.

We need to adopt something like the German distinction between *Wissenschaft*—that is, knowledge or scholarship, which may cover all subjects including chemistry, history, literature, or physics—and *Technik*—the ability to make and use things, whether machine-tools, architectural drawings, or stage-scenery. Such ability may or may not be accompanied by an understanding of the theory that lies behind the skill. That will depend on the particular practitioner.

Though the practical includes the technological, it is wider than that. One of the most obvious practical needs we have is to be able to communicate. We may therefore take as an example of our new dichotomy between the practical and the theoretical the teaching of English. The state of English teaching in schools had obviously, by the late 1980s, become a cause of such radical complaint and discontent that it was not surprising to find a committee of inquiry set up to look into its proper aims and methods (The Kingham Committee, 1987). However highly we may value the findings of this committee, it is worth asserting again the need to distinguish the concept of *language*, as something as necessary to us as our limbs or our most essential man-made tools like spades and kettles, from that of *literature*.

Literature, being a form of art, unlike language, is dispensable. In saying this I do not mean to trivialize art. Far from it. Our highest and most serious imaginative inventions may show themselves in the medium of the arts. And our greatest pleasures may be found there. The very existence of the idea of art, as much as that of language itself, distinguishes man from other animals. Nevertheless there is a distinction to be drawn between the value we must ascribe to language and that which we ascribe to art. Language comes first. We are more seriously cheating children if we fail to teach them how to use language than if we fail to teach them to enjoy and participate in the arts. Besides, those who thoroughly understand the possibilities of their own language are more likely to want to venture into the world of literature than those who have never been taught to have an ear or an eye for language. In the teaching of English, then, I believe that language, the practical aspect of the subject, must have priority and must be distinguished from the theoretical or knowledge-based aspects. We should be prepared to countenance the possibility that there will be children who leave school with little or no literary knowledge; but there should be no children who leave without competence in their own native tongue.

Obviously the teaching of language will involve pupils in reading. But the intention of practical English must be to ensure an understanding of what is read, not necessarily an appreciation of those aspects of it that would appeal especially to literary critics or literary historians. Indeed there are many highly intelligent children who are completely uninterested in the kinds of questions set at O or A level in English, questions about the choice of words in the sonnets of Keats or Jane Austen's power of characterization, who have been set to read these texts with a view to answering such questions, and who are perhaps turned away from reading for ever by being required to embark on a specialized and academic study of literary criticism for which they are totally unsuited by taste, temperament, or ability. Why should we all be critics? It is better that most of us read, if we do, for pleasure.

The dismal nature of English teaching for O and A level in the past can perhaps be accounted for largely by the numbers of pupils entered for the examinations who were not in fact suited to study literature (though they might have benefited from an advanced study of their own language). Teachers have been forced to teach in a way that could be useful to those who had no natural bent for literature at all. Even those pupils who were not entered for any examination have suffered, because teachers have got into a habit of teaching in a particular way, and find it hard to break away from it. Her Majesty's Inspectors in their report on the teaching of English published in 1987 were particularly concerned by the low standard of teaching for A level English: 'Teachers spend too much time scrutinizing past papers and then drilling students in what are taken to be the "correct" answers. Much time is lost because of an assumption that the language of literature is "difficult, mysterious and obscure" and that texts therefore have to be paraphrased line by line and events carefully summarised.'[4] Such dreary teaching could be eliminated if literature were separated from language, theory from practice, and literature became the chosen subject only for those who had a particular aptitude for it, or a desire to learn to criticize and analyse.

By contrast, all of us need to learn how to communicate, and to understand the language we use. Insisting on the primacy of language does not however answer the question *how* the skills of language-using should be taught. Kenneth Baker has been identified with the call to go back to grammar. But 'grammar' is itself an ambiguous pedagogic concept. We would all, I suppose, recognize that to write well and appropriately requires a grammatical sense (as well as a certain number of other abilities). The question is whether grammar ought to be taught as a separate formal study, like harmony or counterpoint, or whether a teacher can assume that it will be picked up through practice. I believe that this is as much a matter of teaching *style* as of a correct single method (it is also a matter of the 'ear' and sensitivity to language of individual pupils). Some teachers may be adept at introducing their pupils to grammatical concepts, or matters of punctuation, by means of jokes and puns which depend on ambiguities, to be cleared up only by distinguishing nouns from adjectives, or different spellings of the same word ('Giant Waves Down Funnel'; 'Gladly the Cross I'd bear' = 'Gladly, the cross-eyed bear', and other well-known punning equivalents, beloved of all children). Others may find a more formal structure easier and more effective. The utility of teaching a foreign language, perhaps especially Latin, as a way of introducing the concepts of tense, parts of speech, and syntactical accuracy should not be underestimated. It has to be remembered that children love an exercise in which they can get things right, or, of course, wrong. Latin grammar and syntax, besides being a ready way to introduce general linguistic concepts, has the great advantage that, at an elementary level at least, it is possible to translate correctly or incorrectly. If you try, you can get ten out of ten. It is no mean achievement. It shows both that you have understood, and that you are capable of accuracy. That there should be a chance for at least some children to learn Latin, not as a part of 'classical studies', but essentially as a branch of linguistic studies, seems to me a benefit that schools should strive to preserve.[5]

But there are many other ways to improve children's accuracy, and therefore full understanding of the possibilities and proprieties of language. For example, Katy Simmonds of the Oxford Polytechnic has described a technique she used with 12-year-old children with specific reading difficulties. She wanted to find out the extent to which children are aware of differences between spoken and written language, of features that might pass muster in speech but not in the written word. She showed these children a series of pictures and got them to tell a story about what they had seen. Their stories were taped and then transcribed verbatim. They then set about correcting stylistic errors and ambiguities in what they had said. She reports that in discussion of the best way to 'tidy up' the stories, children showed considerable awareness of a number of grammatical or syntactical issues. They recognized ambiguity, in cases where, for example, a pronoun might have one of two referents; they recognized syntactical mistakes, as when a character in the story not previously mentioned was introduced as 'the passerby', when the indefinite article would have been appropriate; they quickly spotted mistakes in tense. These children had no formal 'grammatical' vocabulary; but they understood, in a practical way, a good deal about their own language. They knew how it should be used, and could doubtless be taught more and more about how to put this knowledge to good effect. Such latent knowledge is not at all surprising, if we reflect on the amazing complications of the rules of syntax, of constructing intelligible sentences, including the use of tenses, negatives, hypotheticals, which children pick up between the ages of 18 months and 4 or 5, generally without any teaching at all. No one who has heard a 3-year-old, lately able to utter only single words, saying things like 'The difficulty with me is, I don't *want* to go to bed', or 'it looks to me as if my brother has been at it' can fail to toy with a Chomskian or Cartesian notion of innate ideas, the deep structures of language being in us from before birth. A teacher's question is how to tap this latent knowledge, and ensure that pupils take enough care, both in speaking as intelligibly and clearly as in some sense they know how to, and in writing, with the constant aim of criticizing and making less ambiguous whatever they may write. Some teachers will find it essential, in helping children to do this, to use technical terms like 'subject' and 'object'; others will find that such abstract terms of art create a barrier that makes the task more difficult.

Methods however are not so important as outcome. It is fairly easy to reach agreement as to what this should be. It is essential, for example, that school-leavers should be able to write a letter in polite, direct, and simple style, using appropriate formulae to begin and end it. The argument that the use of such formulae, or such a style, is 'mere convention' is no argument. All polite exchanges are conventional to a greater or lesser extent. To say 'good morning' when you first encounter a colleague or employee is a convention, but to fail to do so is none the less offensive. Not to say 'how d'you do' on being introduced to a stranger is equally offensive, though doubtless the greeting is strictly meaningless. I feel genuinely hostile to an undergraduate (supposedly one of the best educated people in the country) who writes asking for sponsorship for some project and who does not know how to begin or end his letter or how to spell the name of the person to whom he is appealing. Such formalities as this are easily taught and can even be fun to teach and learn.

To write accurately and directly, to learn how to tell the truth in writing; to speak clearly and without clichés and fillers (like 'sort of' and 'you know what I mean'); these are skills that can be taught and practised. No one is ever completely a master of his own language. There is always a struggle to get language to do what you want it to; to say, no more and no less, what you want it to say. But it is necessary to start on this battle at school, and it is the duty of teachers to give all the help they can to their pupils to win each engagement.

In a common curriculum, then, everyone ought to study English in this basic, practical, and user-orientated sense, whatever method is used to teach it. Literature, on the other hand, though it may be a popular choice of subject, should be optional. I see no more reason why everyone should read the 'classic' English novels than why everyone should be acquainted with 'classic' English paintings or music. It is very nice to offer pupils at school such cultural knowledge, and to hope that many will take the opportunity to learn (as they are sure to). But for some people literature is a dead-end, just as for some (though I suspect fewer) music is, or the visual arts. Language (the practical) must as a matter of urgency be separated from literature and literary criticism (the theoretical). Otherwise both sides of the subject will suffer.

I have expanded on the teaching of English as exemplifying in a particularly clear way the distinction between the practical and the theoretical. But I might have taken other examples. The distinction is particularly easy to draw in the fields of mathematics, music, electronics, and modern languages, but in history and geography and all the sciences it is essential to draw the distinction as well.

A further reform is necessary. Wherever a pupil is studying the theoretical aspect of a subject, whether in the arts or the sciences, he must be taught to think about the foundations of that subject. Though he will be seeking *Wissenschaft*, he must be taught to relate that knowledge to other knowledge, across a wide spectrum. For years there have been complaints that our school system leads inexorably to too narrow a specialization, especially in the sixth form. There have been numerous attempts to mitigate this evil, from non-compulsory science-for-arts and arts-for-scientists, to the uneasy introduction of AS levels, each worth half an A level, to be taken in a wide variety of different subjects, not necessarily related to the student's main subjects. But as long as the A level system remains, pupils at school will be required severely to limit their choice of subjects, it being assumed that the only way to ensure 'standards of excellence' is to go more and more deeply into an ever narrower range of subjects. The Secretary of State Kenneth Baker set up a committee in 1987, charged with the task of examining A levels (the Higginson Committee). But the terms of reference given to the committee were to see how A levels could be improved, in order that they should remain as 'standards of excellence'. The implication was that A levels must be retained, though, if anything, made slightly harder and more difficult to succeed in. A great chance seems here to have been lost. It would have been opportune for the committee to examine the whole purpose and function of A levels, to see whether they were needed at all; or whether, if retained, they should be radically changed. I shall return to the question of examinations in the next chapter, and to their relation to higher education in Chapter 5.

Whatever the outcome of the Higginson Committee's inquiry may be, if we are to see a radical improvement in secondary education, we must learn to think not merely of a new form of examination (and therefore presumably a novel kind of syllabus that will lead to it) but of a wholly new approach to those studies that we wish to retain in the sixth forms at school, and how these studies are to relate to the pupils' next step, when they leave school. The approach that I have called theoretical as opposed to practical must have as a major part of its aim not merely the passing on of facts and formulae but the inculcation of critical and speculative habit. A pupil who is, for example, studying chemistry, must be encouraged to learn more than certain concepts and procedures. He must be encouraged also to think about the justification, if any, for separating his subject from, say, physics or biology or biochemistry. He must learn how to explain to other people, who are not experts, the concepts which have become familiar to him. He must be able to place his subject both in the context of other academic disciplines and of society as a whole. But, at the same time, these 'philosophical' aspects of his subject must not be a substitute for either accuracy or depth within his chosen field. What is true of chemistry is true of economics, geography, history, and, indeed, of all subjects. We sometimes claim that the merit of an English sixth-form education is that it accustoms pupils to think for themselves. At present there is an ever diminishing justification for such a claim. But the way to make good this promise is, I believe, to take seriously the practical/theoretical distinction and to explore it further. It must be the theoretical aspects of a subject that are employed to encourage free, imaginative thought, speculation, and the conceptual connections between one subject and another, even if in some cases this leads to a breakdown of the divisions between traditional 'subjects'.

The Scottish classicist, educationalist, and philosopher John Burnet once drew a distinction between 'interested' and 'disinterested' knowledge. He argued that 'interested' knowledge, which is knowledge acquired for a particular purpose, is the same as specialist knowledge. It is meant to be put to a specific use. 'Disinterested' knowledge, on the other hand, is essentially generalist. He held that generalist knowledge must take priority; and Scottish schools at the turn of the century were founded on this principle. For it was thought that the generalist could, whenever he wanted to, add a specialist dimension to his knowledge, but general concepts were less easy to derive from the specialist.

Today the word 'general' has a faintly suspect sound. A level 'general studies' has never been taken seriously, certainly not by universities. A general degree is rated lower than any specialist degree, however dismal. Yet there is much to be said for thinking of the general, the 'disinterested', and what I have called the theoretical as one and the same. On the other side of the divide would come the 'interested', the useful, the specialist, and the practical. We may feel that there are just too many dichotomies here for us to cope with. We may become bemused. Never-theless, to line up the specialist with the practical, the theoretical with the generalist may throw light on what should be the future structure of the school curriculum.

It will be objected that what I am suggesting will be the death of 'standards' in schools, and especially in the sixth form. For if general issues concerned with the nature of chemistry or mathematics or history are to take priority, what is to become of the actual content of these subjects? Will not the curriculum inevitably encourage the superficial? We do not want, as our school-leavers, a lot of people who can *talk* about mathematics. We want actual mathematicians. We do not want people who know about structuralism or the 'new criticism'. We want people who have read some literature. There is nothing to be said for propounding the philosophy of history if you do not know the date of the Battle of Waterloo. Such are the arguments. And I concede that any curriculum aiming to cover the theoretical and general aspects of a subject will have to be developed with care. It will have to be backed up by a degree of practical knowledge and competence. Nevertheless, the ideal of the general and the critical needs urgently to be reinstated. We must forget the notion that the highest intellectual achievement is that of specialized and detailed knowledge.

It has to be understood that the general and critical does not mean the vague, the watered-down, or the journalistic. I am not demanding that every subject which has a technical vocabulary or which employs concepts other than those employed by com-mon sense should be rendered simple, and fit for consumption by every man or woman in the street. I do not expect that every teacher and every pupil should adopt the role of the popularizing author or the television-style simplifier of the abstruse. If I, be-ing ignorant, ask a mathematician about his work I must expect, if I am to understand him, to be led into a realm of abstraction that I am unaccustomed to. I shall have to leave the world of concrete numerable objects and follow him into a world of imagination where numbers themselves have discernible charac-teristics, or may hide, waiting to be discovered. I may have to learn a notion of proof different from that to which I am accustomed. But a mathematician should be taught to try to take me with him, so that I may have some appreciation of what he is doing, and why he enjoys doing it.

For there is great danger in the failures of communication consequent on the present A level curriculum. Partly because too many pupils who are not very much interested in the theory are compelled to study it, concepts are introduced that are barely understood, processes are uncritically and mechanically put into operation, unrealistic problems set and solved. There is no time to raise any speculative questions about the interrelation of one part of the curriculum with another.

A more critical approach would inevitably bring about this desirable consequence; it would improve communication. Subject matter has to be made more generally intelligible if it is to be seen no longer as self-contained but as part of a wide and complex body of knowledge. What is needed is an understanding of the principles that lie behind both the selection of questions to be asked, and the methods of supplying answers to them. Whoever thoroughly understands a principle should be able to expound it intelligibly so that other people, non-experts, should understand it as well.

Such a programme for generalizing the curriculum will be attacked, especially by those who distinguish 'difficult' from 'soft' subjects, and who hold that the difficult is the specialized or narrow. Such critics regard an attempt to broaden the base of learning as either a deliberate lowering of standards in the name of equality, or, perhaps, an exercise in politicizing the curriculum. For example, in 1986, when that group of conservatives who called themselves the Hillgate Group published their pamphlet *Whose Schools?*, they set out such fears, and many others, about what they saw as the direction of educational policy in schools. They spoke of 'an increasing displacement of the traditional curriculum in favour of new and artificial subjects'; and they concluded that instead of such 'infantilizing' nonsense, 'the difficult subjects of the traditional curriculum are . . . the thing that is required if a child is to obtain either the competence necessary for a successful adult life, or the wider understanding and enriched experience which are the greatest benefits of education'. And so they went on to recommend a return to selective education at secondary level, with no radical change in the sixth forms of the new grammar schools, even though some of these might be devoted exclusively to science and technology.

Some of the documents reproduced in this pamphlet certainly provide disturbing evidence of the politicization of the curriculum, especially in parts of the ILEA, and to expose this was part of the purpose of the pamphlet. But politicizing the curriculum is not the same (and the authors probably would not suppose it to be the same) as broadening it. Nor is broadening the curriculum in the sense I have suggested the same as 'infantilizing' it, making it 'soft' rather than 'hard'. For though there is a *danger* that a broad curriculum may be superficial, containing nothing but a passing acquaintance with a variety of different subjects, and though this danger must be constantly guarded against, the purpose of the generalized, 'disinterested' curriculum is quite different.

The general or 'philosophical' curriculum that I advocate would be based on a single principle: that the less narrowly a child's critical faculties are confined within the bounds of a single set of concepts or procedures, the more easily he will be able to adapt to life after school, whether at work or in higher education, and the more free his imagination will become; these two targets in fact being one and the same. Most of the detailed factual material learned in the sixth form is forgotten or superseded within a few years. What ought to remain is a technique for learning, and a grasp of intellectual principles that may be applied and reapplied in different circumstances. It seems to me that, in this respect, we have a great deal to learn from the best American schools.

American students emerging from school are far more adept than our school-leavers, even the most academically able, at explaining their subjects, relating their interests to one another over a wide range, and demonstrating some notion of the unity of science. For years we in this country have been accustomed to say 'American education is superficial' or 'the trouble with American students is that they have no idea of scholarship'. But such criticisms become increasingly unconvincing if one observes the enthusiasm with which such students throw themselves into new fields, and make themselves experts, within a short time, in subjects they may never have studied before. Scholarship may come later to them, but when it comes, it has a surer foundation.

It may be asked whether, since a grasp of general principles is what is evidently needed, and an ability to connect together ideas derived from different disciplines, it would not be sensible to teach philosophy as a separate subject at school. For philosophy has just such goals. If pupils at school could study, say, chemistry, physics, and philosophy; or mathematics, music, and philosophy, would they not be on the way to acquiring just that theoretical, critical, and general expertise that is needed? I can see the force of such an argument. Nevertheless I do not believe that philosophy is an appropriate subject for study by pupils at school. Although I advocate what I have called a 'philosophical' approach to particular subjects, I believe that this must be attempted through the study of the subjects themselves. For I do not think it possible to study philosophy profitably without entering fairly deeply into the history of the subject, and for this there is not time at school, nor could it be a subject that would interest more than a very few pupils. Instant philosophy, philosophy that springs into being in the bath or on the television screen, is fun, but can hardly be serious. It would be difficult at school to devote time both to the study of previous philosophers and to the application of philosophy to the current problems thrown up by other subjects. Here there would be a real danger of superficiality. It is preferable for school to be the place to acquire expertise in those subjects which philosophy may later critically examine: mathematics, languages, the physical and biological sciences, art, literature, and history. If all of these subjects were studied at school in a 'generalist' manner, links being forged between one and another, then philosophy itself would greatly benefit, undergraduates at university would be the more ready to study it, and ultimately teachers at school would be better prepared to take what they could from philosophy, and apply it throughout the curriculum.

What we are essentially looking for in secondary education,

then, whether practical or theoretical, is a curriculum and a method of pursuing it that will equip the student with *transferable skills* and *transferable expertise*. A school-leaver may indeed immediately use some of the practical skills he has learned at school, exactly as he has been taught them. If someone has learned how to operate a word-processor or complete an accurate and intelligible technical drawing then it may be that these are skills he can build upon and will not have to relearn. And, of course, in the same way a student going on to university or polytechnic may immediately make use of some of the *Wissenschaft*, the actual knowledge, he has acquired at school. But far more often he will have to turn his hand and his mind to new things; and educationalists, aided both by common sense and the expert knowledge offered by educational psychology, should devote their efforts to providing a school system which will make this possible.

It must be emphasized that the goal of transferability applies equally to the practical and the theoretical, to skills and to knowledge, to arts and to science, and it should be the over-riding aim of school education. Children who never went to school at all would pick up quite a lot of immediately useful knowledge; from television and radio, moreover, they might acquire quite a lot of not obviously useful, relatively esoteric bits of information, about history, for example, or natural history. But such knowledge would not be systematically imparted, with a view of long-term utility, nor with the aim of enabling the student to adapt what he has learned to new and hitherto unthought-of situations. This aim is most likely to be satisfied, in a way that will come nearest to meeting the varying needs of the students, if the distinction between the theoretical and the practical is built firmly into the curriculum, replacing, in the curricular structure, the distinction between arts and sciences. It is crucial that the practical and the theoretical should be given equal weight and equal prestige. Such has been my argument. It is on this principle that the school curriculum should be founded; and this means that no one should leave school without some evidence of achievement in both the practical and the theoretical.

It is relevant here to ask whether such a principle is likely to be honoured in the kind of schools, proposed primarily though not exclusively for the inner cities, to be known as City Technology Colleges. These schools, given a far from warm reception when first proposed, are to be funded in a new way, are to fall altogether outside Local Authority control, and as their name implies are to be devoted primarily to preparing their pupils for a career in industry. Intended as well to improve the educational chances of children in the deprived inner cities, when first proposed they had the somewhat dubious appearance of being the outcome of a bright idea, one that would kill a variety of birds with the same stone: up with the inner cities; down with Local Authorities; up with privatization; down with education in the arts. It is too early to tell how the bright idea may work in practice. But there are clues.

In the original DES document in which the proposals for the schools were outlined[6] the overall aim was said to fit in with the Government's aims set out in their document *Better Schools*,[7] 'to improve standards' being the key phrase. Standards were more likely to be improved, it was said, if parents had a greater choice of schools, and the new Technology Colleges were now to be among the choices on offer for those who lived in their catchment area. For these would be local schools, selecting about 1,000 pupils from an area that contained about 5,000 children of school age, the selection being made in terms of suitability for or ability to benefit from the kind of education to be provided. In addition no child would be admitted at 11 unless his parents undertook to keep him at school until 18 (though presumably the schools would have the right to throw out children who proved unsuitable, or who did not do enough work). Pupils at the new schools would have to expect longer working days and longer terms than at maintained schools. They would have to honour their homework commitments and take part from time to time in residential field trips and work experience courses. They would not have a great choice of subjects in their fourth and fifth years. Throughout their first five years at school, science, mathematics, and design and technology would occupy 50 per cent of their time, the rest being divided between all the arts subjects, including English, and games and PE. In the sixth form they would choose between three or four A levels, or a variety of vocational or practical qualifications in different combinations.

Teachers in these schools are to be the employees of the governing bodies (made up of representatives from the funding industry and of parents) who will be 'free to negotiate pay and conditions of service'. Talking to the Parliamentary Scientific Committee about his new schools in 1987, the Secretary of State expressed himself unworried by the general shortage of teachers in mathematics and the sciences. In these schools, he implied, people would be falling over themselves to get jobs, and, in certain cases, they might be employed even if they had no formal teaching qualifications, though that was not expected to be the norm.

In some ways it is easy to share the enthusiasm of the Secretary of State for his new schools, financially independent (except on the direct grant for students from the DES, paid on a per capita basis), yet with a rigidly controlled curriculum. What, after all, could be wrong with providing at least some good schools in the inner cities, to which parents would be committed and where pupils would have to keep their heads down and work, on pain of being thrown out? But there are two fatal flaws in the scheme, if the arguments I have put forward are right. First, the existence of these private but non-fee-paying schools will have a deeply depressing, if not fatal, effect on other schools in the area, and especially on the science provision in those schools. If certain schools are designated 'science schools' it will be presumed by parents, and indeed by employers and institutions of higher education, that other schools not so designated are weak in science. The consequence will be that they will actually become so. The Local Authority will not think it worth while spending money on science teachers or equipment, nor will properly qualified science teachers be willing to accept posts in such schools.

More fundamentally, the insistence that science and technology are linked together and that schools must concentrate on science at the expense of the arts is a long-term weakness of the scheme. If technology is linked only with science, then vast possibilities in traditional arts subjects will be wasted, and it will be increasingly assumed that modern well-equipped schools are for science, while arts schools struggle along in the doldrums, where neither teachers nor pupils will want to be.

Indeed, the idea of these schools incorporates a division within the secondary curriculum that can only be harmful in the end, and will fail to meet the needs of pupils and of society. All children need to be educated in technology, if this means the practical use of computers, word-processors, and other electronic aids. All children need to be given the chance to create things by means of the new technologies. The crucial distinction to be drawn within the curriculum is, as I have argued, not between arts and sciences but between the practical and the theoretical. All schools must be in a position to teach both of these components.

Before going on to consider how a curriculum so structured should be reflected in an examination system, I must briefly consider another curricular matter. Pupils between the ages of 5 and 16 spend a great deal of their life within the school walls. They are children: they do not know by instinct how to behave and how to treat one another. Ought we, besides equipping them with skills and knowledge, also to teach them good behaviour, good manners, and even good beliefs?

There is no doubt that children learn far more by example than by precept, and therefore that teachers have a continuous obligation to behave well themselves. Parents are anxious that what their children 'pick up' at school should be good example, and in choosing a school they customarily place considerable weight on this kind of consideration. But beyond this most people assume that there will be some actual teaching of such things, and particularly that their children will receive sex education and, by statute, religious instruction. We have to acknowledge, therefore, that the proper balance between the theoretical and the practical is not the only curricular problem with which schools are faced, though it may be the most pressing.

How should these other curricular obligations be faced? Or should we perhaps seize the opportunity, when the whole curriculum is in disarray, to put forward a case for excluding the moral, the social, and the religious from the schoolteacher's sphere of responsibility? Should schools become totally secular, after the French manner? Not only might religious education (and the compulsory school assembly, already more or less a dead letter in many schools) be abandoned, but the obligation to give sex education or moral instruction might also go by the board.

In France teachers, like university professors, come into school simply to teach their own subject. They not only have no obligation to take charge of the moral or spiritual education of their pupils, they have no obligation to help them to develop in aspects of life, such as drama or music, that are not strictly part of their own subject of expertise. It is worth considering the French model since, with the introduction of the national core curriculum, there will be far less time in the school day to devote to non-specialist teaching; and with the new terms and conditions for teachers there may well be many who will want a strict regulation on the number of hours' work they will put in each day.

There is much that is attractive about a French-style rationalization. To take the case of religious education first: in a society that is increasingly mixed in terms of religion and culture and which is in any case predominantly secular, compulsory RE seems an anachronism. It can moreover lead to endless trouble: there are always children who will opt out on parental instructions or with parental permission, or who may be thought to need alternative provision. As the subject has to be studied by all pupils, it tends to become a forum for half-baked discussion of moral or social issues, in order that it may not seem irrelevant to the non-religious, or offensive to the keenly sectarian. In a class devoted to vaguely-worded comparisons between different world religions, or to ill-structured discussion of social and socio-political problems where no examination is taken, there may be a tendency to frivolity both in the preparation of the lessons and in the behaviour of the pupils. And of course such a class lays itself open to prejudice and bias on the part of the teacher, a bias that may be political, racial, or religious.

Such are the arguments in favour of abandoning RE, and by law adopting secularization in a literal sense. On the whole, however, I believe that, though school assembly should cease to be compulsory as an act of worship (largely because it has long ceased to be that anyway), there should be a place in the time-table for the compulsory teaching of Christianity, as long as Church and State are linked. Even in a school where the majority of children practise a faith other than Christianity, something of Christianity should nevertheless be taught.

There was a time when teachers had, above all, to be careful not to speak with the voice of Methodism or Anglo-Catholicism, for fear of offending the sectarian passions of the parents. Now, in contrast, a teacher is more often than not faced with a complete ignorance of Christianity. In many schools the majority of pupils may be practising Jews, Muslims, or Hindus. In many the majority may have no religion at all, and may be totally sceptical about the necessity for there to exist any such thing. For these children the field is wide open to start all over again, and to introduce them to the idea of religion from scratch. If this is to be done, despite the number who are brought up in other religions, it is reasonable to do it largely through the medium of Christianity, simply because Christianity exists as an institution in this country, and is by no means dead. Children will encounter the Christian Church in the outside world, and will meet with Christianity among their contemporaries as they grow up, even if they have not met it at home. But the crucial point is that the history of Christianity is completely interwoven with the history not just of this country but with that of Europe and America as a whole. It is central alike to a study of the arts and of such institutions as the monarchy and Parliament. The educationalist Sir Robert Gould once said that a child being educated in Great Britain could not possibly understand his own environment without understanding something about Christianity; and he was right. But it must be recognized that to teach *about* Christianity though it entails teaching *about* Christian doctrine, with the gospels and at least part of the Old Testament as the source and background of that doctrine, in no sense involves proselytizing. Children are not being taught to *be* Christians.

There is a new attitude towards religion in society, which makes it appropriate and timely to introduce what would, in some ways, be a more serious element into religious education (and indeed this new seriousness is evident in many schools already). RE need no longer be undertaken with the intention of smartening up, or making relevant, something that has become jaded through over-familiarity. On the contrary, it is time to treat religion as something strange and outside the ordinary run of life, something which, mysteriously, has had a vast effect on people, over which wars were fought and people were burned and persecuted, and which still has an effect on people; something which cannot be reduced to mere kindness at the old people's parties or village jumble sales, but which has inspired some of the most splendid painting, writing, music, and architecture ever to be produced by the human imagination, and is still capable of producing martyrdom, cruelty, and sectarian passion. The very unfamiliarity, now, of the language and concepts of Christianity makes it possible to present these anew both as a moral ideal and an attitude to humanity and the capacities of humanity. Moreover, there is, these days, a more sophisticated attitude to the truth. There is a widespread recognition that myth may be a way of illuminating and exploring truth. This makes it possible to present Christianity both as a story and as a part of history, without dogmatism, but also with precision and accuracy. If some children find that the gospels contain truth, then that is well and good. But for those who do not, the phenomenon of Christianity still has to be understood. Whether they love it or hate it, they ought to acquire some knowledge of it. Such new-style RE must be taught by experts, though they need not be theologians. Historians or philosophers would be just as good, provided they were not actually hostile to religion.

Experts are also, and even more crucially, needed for the teaching of 'sex education' classes. It seems to me manifest that in a world in which sexual activity is more and more openly presented in all media, in which sex is exploited for purposes of advertisement and entertainment at every level, and in which people's sexual proclivities are discussed in the plainest terms, children at school need to be given clear information from an early age, and a chance to have their questions answered at various stages of their school career. Most parents want their children to receive sex education at school, and indeed most pupils seem to be reasonably satisfied with what they get. It is far better and essentially less embarrassing for such education to be given at school than within the family, even if it could be certain that parents would give it or that their children would listen. But to conduct such classes well is a difficult business and requires a professional. There is no reason why the biology teacher or the RE teacher should be competent to do it: there is a strong case for peripatetic experts who could be shared between groups of schools.

However, the question how and by whom such elements in the curriculum should be taught is perhaps relatively easily answered. The broader and more difficult question remains. Should teachers at school, like professors at university, be expected in the future simply to teach academic or practical subjects to their pupils, and to have no general pastoral or moral responsibility for them? Sex, religion, PE, music, games, languages . . . whatever was on the curriculum at school would, on such a system, be taught by an expert, but no member of the teaching staff would have more general responsibilities. All would keep strict hours, their duties consisting solely in the preparation and delivery of their lessons. Such a view of the teacher's role would amount to a thoroughgoing 'secularization' of the schools, though not necessarily in a literal sense. For it was the determination to separate State schools from the Church that led, in France, to the establishing of central control over the curriculum, and the employment of teachers by the State as civil servants. As such, it is natural that they should regard their place of work as an office, in which their duties are carried out, but to which they have no other loyalty. French teachers, being civil servants, do not choose their schools; they are posted to them, and may be removed from them and sent elsewhere. It would be professionally improper for them to interest themselves in the social or leisure activities of their pupils; and it would be unsuitable to their professionalism if they were involved in purely supervisory or ancillary duties, which are carried out, where necessary, by unqualified assistants. On this side of the Channel, in contrast, religion still maintains its place in schools, however uneasily; and this itself has made it easier to assume that somehow or other there will be moral teaching as well. Moreover, at least since the nineteenth century there has been a spillover into the State schools of the ethos of the independent boarding schools, the purpose of which was understood to be as much moral as academic, with character-training high on the agenda. And so a strong tradition has grown up that teachers must know their pupils, care for them in a general way, interest themselves in their moral development, and give them as many educational opportunities as possible outside the class-room as well as in it. All schools, maintained day schools as well as private boarding schools, pride themselves on the clubs they support, the plays they put on, the choirs and orchestras they muster. The better the school, the more deeply involved in extra-curricular activities are both pupils and staff. During the time of the teachers' strikes the absence of all these extra-curricular elements of school was regretted as keenly, both by pupils and teachers, as the academic disruption. It was plain then that we did not much like the French way.

With our new spirit of centralization, both as an interim in the matter of teachers' pay and conditions, and in that of the curriculum, and the more general removal of powers from Local Authorities, it may well be that we are imperceptibly going down the French road. I doubt whether there will be a sudden decision in any school that, from today, there will be no more extra-curricular activities, that the choir shall be disbanded, the stamp club wound up. I suspect that such things may gradually wither away, as members of staff are increasingly prepared to give their time according to the letter of their contracts and no more, and are increasingly expected to do so. There will be an ever-widening gap between maintained and private schools, and especially boarding schools, which will have to continue to provide extra-curricular activities, even if they have to pay extra to their staff to enable them to do so. Though not sudden, such changes will amount to a revolution in our schools.

Many teachers themselves will regret the change. There are those whose keenest pleasures in their job are to be found outside the class-room, in informal contacts with their pupils, where they may be able to exercise their own skills or pursue their own hobbies while helping others enjoy the same pleasures. The relation between teachers and their pupils will change, and there are many who will regret the end of a kind of understanding and friendliness that can make teaching itself both easier and more rewarding. Moreover, on the old system where teachers shared responsibility for more than their own lessons, they were brought much more closely into contact with one another, in an informal way. A highly professional teacher in a French school may be very lonely, as undergraduates doing their year abroad as teachers often find. Teaching is more efficient, but not such fun.

Against these drawbacks, however, must be weighed the greater professionalism of teachers on the French model, and thus the greater respect they may be accorded by pupils and parents. A teacher who does nothing but teach and leaves morals, religion, and entertainment to the family and the home is more like an expert, less like a nanny or a parent. Not being *in loco parentis* he can get on with his own job, and expect parents to do theirs.

But many parents are unwilling or unable to accept such a role in the moral or religious education of their children. In Britain, ever since the foundation of the grammar schools in the middle ages, schools have always been thought to have the function of bringing disadvantaged children up to the level of those whose homes are more educative and cultured. If one believes that education is for all children and must be regarded as in many ways the great equalizer, it is hard to accept the proposition that education in morality and religion should be left to parents whose fulfilment of this obligation will be far from equal. It is not only religion and morality that are in question. The thorough 'secularization' of schools would greatly decrease the opportunities children have to participate in drama, music, and sport, enjoyment of which is a crucial part of education.

It is difficult to predict the outcome of changes in the terms of employment of teachers. But if in the maintained schools teachers become more like civil servants, this will afford an additional motive for many parents to move into the independent sector, valuing as many do the overall moral and social responsibility for their pupils that such schools assume. It would be sadly retrograde if the gap between private and maintained schools thus became greater. It may be hard for teachers to combine their professional status with concern for the morals, the welfare, and the 'leisure' development of their pupils. But I believe they will have to try, and will most of them want to do so.

After this digression, it is now time to examine the way in which the curriculum, divided as it should be between the practical and the theoretical, is to be reflected in the school examination system.

Examinations

3

Curriculum reform, whether it is centrally determined or based on local or in-school planning, is generally held to be impossible unless it is firmly based on a plan for public examinations. Some form of pupil assessment, intelligible to everyone and as far as possible uniform throughout the country, is held to be essential since it is through such public assessment that what is taught and learned at school is most clearly related to the world outside school. What employers or universities and polytechnics want of people is encapsulated in the public examinations system, and selection of school-leavers is made predominantly on examination results. People who complain about the failures of schools generally assume such a system, and indeed often judge schools by the examination results that they publish. It is simply taken for granted by the public that curriculum and examinations go together.

There have of course been those who have deplored such a connection. As long ago as 1911 Edmund Holmes wrote of schools that were 'ridden by the examination incubus', arguing that everyone was cheated by a system whose merit-order and pass-lists were nothing but 'outward signs'.[1] More recently there have been frequent criticisms of the injustice of examinations and of their effects on school. Their use as a screen or selector seems to dictate the curriculum rather than merely to reflect it, and to bring it about that easily measurable accomplishments should be given priority, the repeating of acquired factual information, or the mechanical performance of skills picked up without understanding. Methods of teaching as well as the content of the curriculum seem to be determined by the rigid requirements of examinations. When people lament the gap between the imaginative, liberal atmosphere of our primary schools, and the constraints of our secondary schools, they are really lamenting the malign force of public examinations.

Nevertheless we are committed to a meritocratic society. We accept the general proposition that people should rise to the top as far as possible through their talents and skills, not through wealth or influence or inheritance. Moreover we recognize that to talk of 'rising to the top' is an unavoidable metaphor that acknowledges the reality of competition. At some stage in a competition, competitors have to be ranked in order, and this has come to be the role of public examinations. Some form of public assessment, then, has to be accepted. The question is which form will be compatible with the general curriculum aims set out in the last chapter. We need a system of assessment that will encourage, not inhibit, the development of the imagination, and the new emphasis on practical skills as of equal importance with scholarship and learning. What has to be examined is transferable expertise, both in the practical and the theoretical senses of the term.

It may still be objected that, though pupils at school must be in some way ranked in order of merit, the only way to do this that would not be restrictive is by in-school assessment. Teachers within each school should be trained to make their own formal reports on their pupils, and these should form the basis of selection, whether by employers or by universities and polytechnics. There is indeed a considerable movement in this direction, so-called 'profiling' being increasingly undertaken by schools, often with the active co-operation of pupils themselves.

The movement could be said to have started in Scotland in 1972, when the Headteachers' Association set themselves to determine the range of items of information needed to produce a comprehensive picture of the aptitudes and interests of all pupils, offering them a common form of statement, which would be generally comprehensible and would be available to them when appropriate. Since 1977 numerous schemes have been introduced in England and Wales. In Wales there is a nationally agreed pupil profile; and many groups of schools or Local Authorities in England have been working on forms of profiling that would be objective and intelligible. In 1987 Neal Ascherson wrote an article in the *Observer* about 'a document circulating in the Department of Education' which suggested a 'quite new' way of assessing performance, not by examination results but by behaviour. 'Figures for truanting, lateness and absenteeism will . . . be fed into the computer. So will the proportion of pupils taking part in extra-curricular activities . . . Local opinion on how the pupils look and behave on their way to and from school will be another indicator.'[2] This so-called 'secret' document is concerned with methods of assessing schools, and determining which are 'value for money' and which are not. But the method proposed goes hand in hand with the method of assessing individuals by profiling.

There are two related objections to such a system of assessment. The first is that of credibility. A report on a pupil from within his own school will never be generally regarded as adequate, however conscientiously compiled. Individual schools and individual teachers differ widely from one another, not least in the expectations they hold of their pupils. In one sense, like parents, teachers know their pupils too well. In another sense they may seem to know them too little, to be too little able to see them in relation to other, contemporary, young people: as much chance of a fair assessment from a family as from a school.

Even if the keeping of profile records were somehow formalized and given a common validity, there is a related and more serious danger. In 1984 David Hargreaves, formerly Chief Inspector in ILEA and now Professor of Education at Cambridge, called attention to this danger in a paper entitled 'Motivation versus selection: a dilemma for Records of Achievement' (1986). He raised the question whether teachers ought to

mediate employer values by encouraging pupils to record only those activities and achievements which call to mind such things as loyalty, dependability and leadership . . . scouting and guiding, playing in the school orchestra, running the fishing club, for instance? And how do they react to those activities which might not chime so sweetly in the ears of employers . . . to Rastafarianism, feminism, peace campaigning or the like? Do they discourage pupils from recording achievements of these kinds, and what would be the consequence of his denial of experience for a pupil's sense of worth and motivation?

There is in fact a general danger that 'good' records will turn out to look remarkably similar to one another, 'bad' records made up only for non-comformists, individualists, or those who are in some way social or school 'loners'. An insidious and intrusive pressure may be laid on pupils which, under the guise of a friendly and honest account of a pupil's interests and activities, may prove just as much of a turn-off for the imaginative or deviant as the examination system itself, and may come quite soon to be regarded with cynicism by both pupils and employers alike.

There is a further drawback. Although Sir Frederick Dainton, formerly a chairman of the University Grants Committee, spoke in 1984 of the need for a 'global, school-based assessment including profiles to end universities' reliance on A levels' for their admissions selection, it is exceedingly unlikely that entry to higher education would ever come to rely on profiles, or any other in-school method of assessment alone. Thus profiling is always likely to be seen as of peripheral importance to the academically able, central only to those who have already been deemed unsuitable for further or higher education. The 'profiles' school-leaver would thus take his place among the list of the failures, whether designated as 'secondary modern' school-leavers, the educationally subnormal, the 'bottom 40 per cent', or by whatever other title the no-hopers are characterized.

In her article 'Alternatives to Public Examinations', Patricia Broadfoot of Bristol University has drawn an interesting parallel between 'profiling' and the new French system of 'orientation', according to which pupils at school are continuously assessed by teachers and, with parental co-operation and pupil participation, are guided in the direction of suitable curricular goals. The system was introduced in order to counter the lack of motivation and the crippling sense of failure among school students engendered by the fiercely competitive and academic Baccalauréat examinations. But now to be 'orientated' is widely seen not as helpful guidance but as a test one has to submit to. Its outcome is still a division between the sheep and the goats. Patricia Broadfoot comments,

Orientation operates in much the same way as the intelligence test used to . . . its particular value being that its apparent scientific objectivity made it an excellent means of justifying selection. Thus orientation conceals under a pretence of 'equal but different' a process of sorting and selecting pupils according to their academic level for different scholastic and ultimately occupational routes.[3]

I am convinced that pupil-profiling alone cannot be the way forward, even if profiles may profitably be used in conjunction with other methods of assessment. There have been numerous suggestions over the years that profiles or school reports should be used in conjunction with examination results. In 1943 the Norwood Report put forward such a suggestion,[4] which was repeated in the report of the Secondary Schools Examination Council in 1947, and by the Crowther Report in 1959.[5] But the more profiles are concerned with qualities of character and extra-curricular activities, the more intrusive of privacy they seem; and, perhaps more relevant to the present enquiry, the less they have to do with the actual school curriculum. What is needed is a public examination system based outside school, which will act as an incentive, not an inhibition, to curricular reform, and will as far as is possible assess pupils accurately, without at too early a stage designating some as 'non-examinable' or beyond the educational pale. A curriculum that genuinely values the practical as highly as the theoretical or academic must be geared to a public assessment system that does the same, and from which only the severely mentally handicapped, and not all of them, will need to be totally excluded.

How near are we to such a system? It is time to turn to the turbulent scene of public examinations as they now are. The first GCE O and A level examinations were held in 1951 (S levels were at that time an essential part of the system as well, since on them depended the award of State scholarships to university candidates, before the days of mandatory awards). In 1958 the Beloe committee was set up to examine public secondary school examinations other than the GCE, and as a result of the Beloe report, published in 1960, CSE examinations were instituted on a regional basis and with strong teacher involvement, primarily to serve the needs of the secondary modern schools. The first of these examinations were held in 1965. An overlap of the two otherwise distinct systems was allowed, in that a Grade 1 at CSE was permitted to count as an O level pass in that subject. The pattern of two parallel systems of subject-based examinations (that is, where passes in individual subjects could be achieved) has persisted until 1988, when the first examinations in the new CSE at 16+ were held.

There are two major innovations incorporated in the new General Certificate of Secondary Education. In the first place it is a single system of examinations in place of the dual system that has been operating for the last twenty-two years. There have been frequent demands for a single system and investigations of its possibility; for after the introduction and spread of comprehensive schools it was clearly both inconvenient and divisive that pupils within the same school should be classified either as fit to take the GCE or fit only for the CSE. Teachers had to make this distinction at the end of the third year, or earlier. They were under strong pressure, especially from parents, to enter children for the GCE, and frequently the reputation of a school turned on the numbers of candidates who were entered and passed in the O level examinations. But to fail at O level might mean that a child ended with nothing at all to show for his time at school. Therefore there were numerous double-entries for both O level and CSE, a procedure that was expensive and confusing. A single system for all seemed an obvious solution to such problems. Pupils themselves disliked the way that they had previously been divided from one another; and although there had been considerable advances made in the early 1980s in running joint CSE/GCE courses and examinations, these were patchy and voluntary, and unlikely to have been acceptable to the more academic of those who had an interest in the outcome of the examinations, especially the universities.

The second major innovation incorporated in the GCSE is that it is supposed to be marked by 'criteria reference' rather than 'norm reference'. In the case of the GCE, both at O and at A level, maximum possible marks were allocated to each question on the examination papers before the papers were written, and there were cut-off points in total marks, determining the different grades. Roughly the same proportion of pupils gained each grade each year, the proportions more or less determined by past years. Thus in A level, roughly 30 per cent of candidates will fail, in O level about half of those entered obtained D or E grades or were totally unclassified. This inevitably led to a sense of frustration both in pupils and their teachers; for it seemed that however well taught they were, however much they learned, it was inevitable that a high proportion of candidates would get low or unclassified grades. Criteria referencing, on the other hand, looks in the written scripts for evidence of what the candidates actually know and can do, and marks are allocated on these grounds. There is therefore reference in the case of each candidate to his own positive ability, not to the whole class of other candidates with whom he is to be compared. In principle on such a scheme it would be possible for every candidate to get a pass mark, or indeed to get the highest grade. It would be equally possible, in principle, for all to fail. The Secondary Examinations Council, established in 1984 to introduce the new-style exam, set out in its published *General Criteria* (1985) its commitment to this philosophy, to a system that would demonstrate what candidates 'know, understand and can do'. This constitutes a revolution that has, I believe, been very generally welcomed.

The criterion-basis of the new examination seemed to open up the possibility of an assessment system that would be public, open, and uniform, yet applicable to virtually all pupils in school, whatever their ability. Thus it was welcomed because it seemed to bring together on the one hand the idealized liberalism of the 1960s and 1970s—when pupils and teachers hoped to romp together through an uninhibited dance of individualized learning, projects, pupil-centred learning-situations, and an end to authoritarian concepts of knowledge—with, on the other hand, the 1980s demand for 'standards'. The question has to be raised, however, whether such an unlikely marriage of opposite ideals has worked, or could possibly work.

The new examination consists of a combination of course-work, assessed by teachers, and final examinations to be taken in a block at the end of the two-year course. This is not a radical change, though it has sometimes been represented as such. Many schools have used continuous assessment of course-work as part of the work leading to GCE O level (Mode 3); and still more have used it in the CSE examinations. It is only those schools that have been predominantly academic, and independent schools which have seldom tangled with CSE or Mode 3 levels that may find it new. The purpose of course-work assessment in the GCSE was summed up by the Secondary Examination Council's 1985 publication: the overall aim was 'to make what is important measurable, not what is measurable important'. But admirable as this *bon mot* may be, the widespread use of the necessary techniques is causing some anxiety. In an article entitled 'Course-work', Tim Horton writes 'the problems of storing, retrieving and analysing course-work marks could impose an enormous organisational burden on schools. The paucity of administrative support staff, particularly at departmental and faculty level in secondary schools will be increasingly exposed.'[6]

Moreover teachers have to decide how often and at what stages to assess their pupils' work. This is a difficulty shared by all course-work assessment schemes at whatever level. If the final grade is largely determined by course-work marks, how are you to mark a piece of work completed in a pupil's first term of his introduction to a subject, compared with what he can do after five or six terms? Are his first fumbling efforts to compose an essay on the history of the bathing machine to be marked on the same scale as his final polished piece in term 6 on 'The Economic Significance of the English Watering Place'? The early efforts are not meant to be marked on promise alone; yet it is hard not to do that. It is such considerations of equity and judgement that make the course-work component in examinations suspect, however much its assessment may be regulated by published sets of criteria.

A more fundamental difficulty with the new examination is contained in the very principle that made it at first sight so attractive—its applicability to the full ability range. The Secondary Examinations Council has been insistent that the new examination is not geared to any particular percentage of the ability range, as O level and even CSE were. It is hoped that as many as 90 per cent of all school children will take part. In the DES introductory booklet to the GCSE (1985) the point is made somewhat confusingly:

The standards required of successful candidates in GCSE examinations will not be less exacting, grade for grade, than those required in the existing GCE and CSE examinations. They will be designed not for any particular proportion of the ability range but for all candidates whatever their ability relative to other candidates who are able to reach the standards required for the award of particular grades in each subject. The Government seeks a progressive raising of standards of attainment. As and when this happens the proportion of pupils obtaining graded results will naturally be greater in the GCSE than in the existing examinations.

There are seven grades to be allotted, from A to G. Grades A, B, and C are aligned to the old O level grades A, B, and C, and to CSE grade 1. Grades D and E are aligned to O level grades D and E and to CSE 2 and 3; while grade F is aligned to CSE grade 4, which used to be considered the average grade in the population as a whole. Grade G is aligned to CSE grade 5 (below average) and there is an unclassified grade below G.

Presumably this lining-up of grades, with equivalents in the old O level and CSE grading system, was undertaken in order to reassure people that 'standards' were going to be as rigorous as before. Perhaps there was a wish also to demonstrate that what was on offer was a genuinely single system, combining both of the old systems of examination. But this has not been a wholly successful operation. GCE O level and CSE were designed to be wholly different kinds of examinations. Though CSE grade 1 had been deemed to be the equivalent of a good O level pass, this had not really brought the two into line: the equivalence was granted as a concession to the increasingly academic ambitions of the secondary modern schools, and, later, as a consolation to those pupils in comprehensive schools who thought they had been wrongly 'deselected' away from O levels. It was a way of remedying possible mistakes. But there had never been any attempt to align other CSE grades to O level grades and it was no part of the assumptions of the dual system that someone who failed O level (below grade E) was of 'average' ability (CSE grade 4). It is peculiarly unfortunate for the new examination that grade F, the next to bottom grade, should come out as 'average'. Such an equivalence suggests, perhaps wrongly, that most candidates in comprehensive schools will be expected to do no better than score an F or a G in their GCSE. This would not matter very much (for it would always be possible for individual candidates to prove the expectation wrong), if it were not for the fact that whole papers in the final examination, or certain questions on papers, are to be 'differentiated'. They are to be divided into the 'easy' and the 'difficult'. Thus it may soon come about (may indeed have come about already) that teachers will be advising 'average' pupils not to attempt the difficult questions; or will separate them out to sit special papers suitable only for the F grades. In this way F must soon be interpreted as standing for 'Fail'.

The differentiation within the examination is to be carried out according to strict criteria, laying down in detail what the candidate is expected to know, understand, and be able to do. According to these expectations some whole papers will be 'lower' than others, some individual questions picked out and designated 'lower'. The criteria are, of course, different according to the varied subject matter of the examination. But it is perhaps worth looking at part of one fairly characteristic set. The criteria are supposed to define the main area of knowledge and understanding, and to specify the skills and competences to be tested in each subject. How this is done relatively to the subject and the grades will be clear if we look at some of the grade criteria for history, published in 1985.

At grade C (one of the top grades) a candidate must first of all be able

to recall and use historical knowledge accurately and relevantly in support of a logical and evaluative argument; to distinguish between the cause and the occasion of an event; to show that change in history is not necessarily linear or progressive; to compare and contrast people, events, issues and institutions; to demonstrate understanding of such concepts by deploying accurate though limited evidence.

At grade F (the 'average' grade), in contrast, as a start a candidate must be able

to recall and display a limited amount of accurate and relevant historical knowledge; to show a basic understanding of the historical concepts of cause and consequence, continuity and change, sufficiently supported by obvious examples; to identify and list differences and similarities.

At grade C the next requirement is that the candidate should be able 'to show an ability to look at events and issues from the perspective of other people in the past; to understand the importance of looking for motives'. At grade F, in contrast, the candidate is required 'to display knowledge of perspectives of other people based on specific examples of situations and events'.

After various other criteria, we come at last to the manner in which this knowledge and understanding must be expressed. At grade C a candidate must be able to 'communicate clearly in a substantially accurate manner, making correct and appropriate use of historical terminology', whereas the F grade candidate must do no more than 'communicate in an understandable form, and use simple historical terminology'.

Such differing criteria as these will presumably be used for the purpose of assessing the course-work component of the examinations as well as the final papers. It must also be presumed that gradually over the years some kind of folklore will develop, a collective consensus about how to apply the criteria to the actual written work to be examined, whether as course-work or examination scripts. For at first it looks an extremely daunting task.

The good candidate, for example, must distinguish between 'cause' and 'occasion'; the average candidate, on the other hand, must show an understanding, albeit basic, of the concepts of 'cause' and 'consequence'. It seems to me hard to do the latter without being able to do the former. The average candidate has to understand the concepts of continuity and change; it is only the good candidate who has to believe and demonstrate that 'change is not always linear' (whatever that may mean). But if it is true that change is not always linear, then surely even the average candidate must know this, if he is to understand the concept of change. However, it is at the end of the list of criteria that the real difference between the poor F candidate and C becomes clear. What F writes need be no more than barely 'understandable', provided that he throws in from time to time some 'historical terminology', which he need not necessarily understand, nor use appropriately. C, on the other hand, has to be clear and reasonably accurate; and for him the historical terminology must be correctly used.

There is a real difficulty here. What is the difference between a candidate who performs inadequately, though he tackles quite difficult questions, and one who performs well though he tackles only specially selected easy questions, questions that do not for example raise any issue about linear or non-linear, progressive or retrogressive change? If an F-type candidate is identified in time by his teacher, he may be entered for an F-type examination and may thus at least be saved from getting a G grade or worse. But a candidate not so ear-marked may sink to an F or G anyway when it is found that his language though intelligible is not accurate, or that though he knows some historical terminology he uses it inappropriately. But on what grounds will a teacher identify a pupil as F, and put him in for the F exam? He will presumably be picked out on his course-work. But his course-work ought not to be *irredeemably* F. If the teacher is any good, he should be teaching his pupils all the time, so as to improve their historical understanding and their powers of accurate expression, to raise them from F to E and D and beyond. It is very likely, in fact, that a teacher will designate a pupil an F pupil on some very general and intuitive grounds rather than in accordance with any strict criteria. Indeed, such vaguely formulated judgements seem inescapable: 'He's just not very bright', 'He's practically illiterate', and other such familiar characterizations. Of course the problems of distinguishing F from C, goat from sheep, are no worse than the problems teachers were faced with for years, when they had to separate O level candidates from those who would work for CSE. But I suggest that though the problems are no worse, they are not much better either. In an article in the *Guardian* in 1986 J. Matthew made the same point: 'This is little different from the GCE/CSE dual system, except that the segregation will be hidden, all certificates being headed GCSE.'

Those who hoped, then, for a genuinely unitary system of examining may be disappointed (though it is far from clear that their hopes were ever realistic). Such revolutionaries also complain that by adhering so closely to the old subject divisions, in the past characteristic more of GCE O levels than of the CSE, those who devised the new examination missed a great opportunity. For it would have been possible, they argue, to move towards a system that examined knowledge and skills which crossed old subject boundaries; a new way of looking both at the sciences and the arts could have been incorporated in the new syllabuses. In this I believe they are right. The more time we have had to consider the GCSE, the less revolutionary in any true sense it seems to be.

But one has to remember the difficulties, in practical terms, of introducing genuinely new ideas into education, an area bound to be in part wedded to tradition and the conservation of the old. One must remember too that the authors of many of the changes we now see have been Conservative Secretaries of State. Keith Joseph and Kenneth Baker, though I believe they are genuinely anxious to improve the lot of all children at school, have nevertheless been subject to pressure from the most inflexibly conservative thinkers. Professor Roger Scruton, for example, is a philosopher greatly revered by the Conservative party, whose views cannot be lightly set aside by Conservative ministers. His hand was obvious in the writing of the pamphlet *Whose Schools?* In November 1986 he wrote an article in *The Times* specifically about the effect of GCSE on those pupils who wanted to proceed to university. He started in rousing style: 'Education in England and Wales has suffered many catastrophes in recent years but none so great as the new GCSE examination. For the first time the egalitarian mentality has been able to impose its will not only on the State schools, but on the private schools.' 'The GCSE', he continues, 'with its emphasis on "course-work", "continuous assessment" and "transferable personal skills" is designed to minimize the distinction between academically gifted children and the others. Its purpose is not to discriminate but to "differentiate", not to assess but to destroy the possibility of assessment.' He goes on to deplore the abandonment of 'subjects that really matter', and the exchange of 'solid fact' for 'airy speculation'. Nothing would satisfy him, he implies, but a return to the old ways, for only so can academic standards be maintained. We shall consider in a moment the grip this kind of thinking has on the conservative mind, not merely the politically Conservative, but traditionalists of all kinds.

But before turning to this, and the related topic of the A level examination, it is necessary to consider some of the other influences at work on a reforming Secretary of State and his Department. These influences are strong, and often contradictory. For besides the radical conservatism and traditionalism of Roger Scruton, politicians are also moved increasingly by a distrust of the universities. It has often been pointed out, and in my view with justice, that the school curriculum has in the past been overwhelmingly in the power of the universities. This has been in part because the universities have a perfectly general responsibility for disseminating among schools up-to-date advances in knowledge and theoretical changes within disciplines, but also, more specifically, through the Local Examination Boards they have been in a position to determine the syllabuses for public examinations, and so to a large extent to dictate a curriculum even for those pupils at school who may never themselves enter the door of a university.

For those who were destined for university, for whom A levels and S levels were first invented, they could go even further. They could dictate not only the content of particular syllabuses, but the combination of A levels that would be acceptable to university faculties. Medical and veterinary faculties (for which the competition was high, the numbers limited) could lay down that candidates would not be considered unless they got high grades in physics, chemistry and biology at A level. This entailed that the three subjects were for ever to be treated as three separate subjects. Moreover, since it came to be accepted by many schools that a pupil could not study these separate subjects at A level unless he or she had already studied them at O level (although in the 1950s it had been intended that O levels should be 'bypassed' by those who would study a subject at A level) the domination of the university faculties began when a pupil was 14. Radical changes in the nature of individual separate 'subjects', and serious attempts to widen the scope of a pupil's education at school were virtually blocked by the universities.

The absurdity of the universities' power to dictate the curriculum to schools catering for children, 90 per cent of whom were not proceeding to university, was manifest. It was part of the failure of the comprehensive schools to shake off the image of 'grammar schools for all'. The introduction of the CSE was, however, an important step in the direction of freeing schools from this thrall. The CSE boards were not university dominated. It is possible to see the introduction of the GCSE as a much more dramatic step in the same direction. At a time when the universities were widely regarded by politicians as idle, expensive, and impervious to the demands of vocationalism in education, such a step was welcome and, indeed, government-inspired. Good schools would educate their pupils to be useful, practical, and self-motivated. Universities were genuinely held to have little legitimate right to say how this should be done. Part of the power behind the GCSE, then, was teacher power; schools, not universities, determining the curriculum.

But there was a much more important shift of power away from the examining boards (and thus away from the universities) in the creation of the central Secondary Examinations Council. It was this Council, consisting of members nominated by the Secretary of State himself, who issued the National Criteria according to which the new examination should be conducted, and who continue to approve all the particular subject criteria, which must be finally approved by the Secretary of State. Thus, in the end, through the SEC, there is central control. The examination boards, newly grouped on broadly regional lines, are responsible for administering the examinations, but no longer for determining the syllabuses or the methods of examination. The new system could be said to depend on a principle of school-based centralization.

The GCSE system as a whole has already made an enormous difference to teaching methods in schools. Pupils' work is generally expected to be more practical, the oral being regarded as of the same importance as the written. Pupils themselves have to take much more responsibility for the work they do. Indeed, they are treated more as grown-up students than as children to be spoon-fed, and this in almost every case has a good effect both on the work produced and on their motivation. For example, in art, pupils have to hand in work to be assessed throughout the course, and they can thus accumulate a varied and impressive portfolio as part of their examination achievement. In the same way, in geography and biology records of field-work form the most important part of the examination, enthusiasm and imagination being properly rewarded. Teachers have had to adapt to the need to allow their pupils this kind of responsibility and self-propulsion, and for those who have been accustomed to telling their pupils in detail how to defeat the examiners on the fateful day, this has been a great change. The organization of field-work has proved tremendously time-consuming for teachers, and the complications of a timetable so predominantly practical and involving so much more experimentation and research on the part of the pupils have not always been overcome. There is greater demand in every school for time, space, and equipment. The problems may be overcome, but not without considerable expenditure.

In some subjects these new methods have led to so radical a change in the content of the syllabus that the effects will necessarily be felt in the sixth form and in all further and higher education. One obvious example of such changes is in the teaching of languages. The syllabus for modern languages in the GCSE is very full; but there is no place in it for the teaching of grammar. In the case of an inflected language or one with many and various verb-forms, it has been almost impossible for teachers to adapt to the new methods. In any case, if any of the pupils are to go on with the language at A level, they will simply have to learn some grammar at some stage. The full effects of the new language-teaching have yet to be felt.

The GCSE, in short, though in many ways an exciting new development, represents an uneasy compromise. It attempts to be a proof that all children can be educated; yet it is also supposed to form a preparation for higher education to which only a few will aspire. It attempts to be a preparation for A level, while also satisfying the new demands for a practical education, accessible to everyone. It is doubtful whether any system could succeed in these contradictory aims.

However, the demand for the relevant, the practical, and the vocational that was part of the *raison d'être* of the GCSE has at the same time been answered in a different way, which may in the end prove embarrassing to the DES and the SEC, and may seem to promise yet another shift of power. In an article entitled 'GCSE and the new Vocationalism' Ian McNay of the Open University writes:

To those committed to a relevant as well as a rigorous education, the GCSE is a disappointing anachronism which doesn't fit with vocational or pre-vocational criteria exemplified through other contemporary school-based developments for 14–18-year-olds such as TVEI (Technical and Vocational Educational Initiative) and CPVE (Certificate of Pre-Vocational Education).

And he adds that the GCSE can be seen 'as a final attempt to adjust the classical approach [to education] to cater for everybody . . . before the instrumental barbarian hordes establish an alternative empire'.[7] I referred in Chapter 2 to the firm place in the curriculum now occupied by the TVEI scheme, and to the 1986 Government White Paper *Working Together: Education and Training*. It seems that there is a genuine unclarity in Government thinking about the connections, if any, between this scheme (run and financed, it will be recalled, not by the DES but by the Manpower Services Commission (now Training Commission) under the Department of Trade and Industry) and the GCSE.

One might hope to find enlightenment on this in the brochure issued by the DES in 1986, setting out the principles of Kenneth Baker's brain-child, the City Technology Colleges. For surely there, if anywhere, there should be the optimum mix of vocational with academic, and common examinations for all. But in years 4 and 5, the years that in other schools would be devoted to working for the GCSE with continuously assessed coursework, and when the TVEI scheme would also be introduced, we are told nothing whatever about examinations, only that the pupils will not have a wide choice of subjects. It is only in the sixth form, apparently, that pupils will work for examinations.

This may be a simple oversight on the part of the authors of the pamphlet, or it may reflect the thought that since those who attend these colleges would have committed themselves to staying at them until they were 18 (and such a commitment would be a condition of entry), there would be no need for them to take a 'school-leaving' examination at 16 +.

The sixth-form course in the City Technology Colleges is envisaged as generally lasting for two years. The two-year course may lead to A levels; but other courses may lead to a variety of qualifications: BTEC, City and Guilds, GCSE, or the Certificate of Pre-vocational Education. There is thus a proliferation of public examinations of a practical kind, any of which may be taken at the new schools, of which the GCSE seems to be only one, if it is to be taken at all.

In July 1986, while the DES was busy finalizing plans for the introduction of the GCSE, a new body was established under the aegis of the Department of Employment, named The National Council for Vocational Qualifications. The aim of this Council was presumably to rationalize post-16 vocational provision, and establish criteria according to which the various existing qualifications may be accredited in a uniform way. The bodies that will come together to be unified are the Joint Board for the City and Guilds of London Institute (CGLI), the Business and Technical Education Council (BTEC), and the Royal Society of Arts (RSA). The Certificate of Pre-vocational Education would fall to be accredited within this overall scheme, and is an especially interesting innovation. It was certified for the first time in 1986. It has a strong emphasis on specific objectives (related to a number of vocational choices to be made by the students themselves), to cross-curricular skills and to profile-reporting on progress. There is a determination displayed within the guidelines to assess what a student can do; and the academic distinction between traditional subjects has been virtually eliminated. In many ways the CPVE conforms very closely to the goals originally set out for the GCSE. But because the conception of the Certificate did not originate within the recognized schools examination boards, indeed had nothing to do with the DES, it is now thought of as suitable more for further education than for schools, and it seems to invoke all over again the old distinction between 'education' and 'training'. But it is certainly cited as one of the examinations that pupils at the new Technology Colleges may take.

All this is not very encouraging for those who want to see the GCSE as a single simple examination system catering for virtually all school pupils according to their needs. In future it seems quite likely that there may be pressure from the Training Commission for a test or certificate of attainment specifically for those working on the TVEI, and that certificate might overlap with the Certificate of Pre-vocational Education. But since work for the TVEI starts at the age of 14, two years before the GCSE is to be taken, it is not clear how that examination will fit in; for it is not yet certain how much vocationalism can be accommodated within the GCSE itself. Moreover, where science is concerned, the GCSE (and certainly A levels) has so far been mainly committed to separate sciences, biology, chemistry, and physics, according to the traditional pattern. The TVEI scheme, on the other hand, is more concerned with problem-solving across all the sciences. It may thus be difficult for the two schemes to be made compatible. As to this we must wait and see.

The final phase of academic school examinations, as distinct from the vocational examinations already mentioned, is, and seems likely to remain for the foreseeable future, the GCE A level. A levels have been the subject of considerable criticism over the years, but there have been few serious demands that they should be replaced. They are indeed a species of sacred cow. They are seen as the last defence of standards. My own belief, for which I shall attempt to argue, is that, whatever may become of the GCSE (and its future seems very speculative), A levels should gradually be made redundant. The greater the variety of non-academic and pre-vocational examinations there are on offer, the easier it may be to progress in this direction. Now is certainly the time for fundamental reform.

Since the introduction of A levels, English, Welsh, and Northern Irish schools, unlike schools in Scotland, Europe, or America, have expected pupils to study at most three examinable subjects in their years in the sixth form, these three being generally either all arts or all science subjects, though mathematics has been found commonly on either side of the divide. Apart from the three subjects intensively taught, pupils may make up their timetables with scraps of non-examined, and therefore non-serious, odds and ends. Such has been the normal pattern.

The effect of such narrow specialization in subject content and style of teaching has already been remarked on. There have been various attempts to broaden the sixth-form curriculum, none of which has been successful. The latest, which has now been introduced on a voluntary basis, is that, instead of one of his A levels, a pupil may take two AS (supplementary) level examinations, demanding half the time each of a full A level. In principle this might seem satisfactory. But shortage of teachers and timetabling problems make it very difficult for schools to work any great breadth into the system. Too often an AS level is simply half an A level. Whether to study two half-syllabuses in place of one whole one is a rational procedure is extremely dubious. In any case the universities, while all through the 1960s, 1970s, and 1980s publicly deploring the undue specialization of the English sixth form, nevertheless for the most part continue to demand it, especially of those candidates who wish to read science or languages.

In the days of the Schools Council, a body largely controlled by teachers and concerned with curricular innovation, there were several suggestions for the reform of the sixth-form curriculum. But these were never acceptable to the universities. Moreover, the Council itself was widely regarded as dangerously left-wing, dominated not just by teachers, but by teachers acceptable to the furthest left of the teachers' unions, the NUT (itself then containing a large proportion of primary school teachers, without university connections). So there were many, even among teachers, who, being university orientated, did not care for the Council. When the Council was wound up in 1982, being replaced by the Secondary Examinations Council and School Curriculum Development Committee, there was so much work to be done on the curriculum and the examination of it in the years of compulsory school that consideration of the sixth-form curriculum lapsed into comparative inertia.

In any case the real difficulty has always been the use of A levels as a selection examination by the universities and polytechnics. The degree of collaboration between secondary and higher education, if any reform is to be envisaged, must always be daunting. Yet unless such collaboration is forthcoming I see little hope of any genuine improvement in our education. New curricular ideals need new public examinations. But such examinations must be adapted not only to the past (what the candidate has actually learned at school) but to the future (what he will have to learn, understand, and be able to do next). We need to consider a form of examination that can reflect the ideal of 'transferable skills', and of the equal importance of the practical with the theoretical, that can above all reflect the ideal of broad 'philosophical' understanding within each subject-area, which can come to be respected by those concerned with selection for higher education as an indicator of potential achievement. A levels as at present constituted do not meet these needs.

However, as we have seen, central government, who through the SEC has boldly pressed on with the introduction of the GCSE, has even in doing so been subject to its own and its advisers' demands that Standards should be preserved. The whole exercise, indeed, was largely dictated by the very proper wish to see standards of education rise. Any suggestion that A levels should be changed has been strongly resisted on the ground that this would inevitably lower standards. Even though the universities, through the Committee of Vice-Chancellors and Principals, early expressed themselves willing to consider radical changes in their own admissions procedures and demands, A levels have been regarded by Government as sacred. Any change would be open to the charge that it constituted a further 'infantalization' of the examination system. Indeed in *The Times* article already quoted Roger Scruton was particularly scornful of the Vice-Chancellors for their apparent readiness to change: they were accused of being interested only in the quantity, not the quality, of students; and of being happy to lower their standards, and offer as items in university courses 'subjects' which have no proved intellectual value. In this spirit, and doubtless moved by these very arguments, early in 1987 Kenneth Baker set up his committee under the chairmanship of G. R. Higginson, the Vice-Chancellor of Southampton University, to recommend principles that should govern A level syllabuses and their assessment 'in the light of the Government's commitment to retain GCE Advanced level examinations as an essential means for setting standards of excellence, and with the aim of maintaining or improving the present character and rigorous standards of these examinations'. Seldom can a Committee of Inquiry have been told more firmly what they had to do, and what they might *not* do.

After this bold statement of intention, the Secretary of State, in subsequent instructions to the newly formed committee, showed some awareness of the contradictory requirements of a satisfactory 18 + examination. He spoke of a syllabus that would demand breadth and balance of knowledge and understanding, without any sacrifice of depth of study. He mentioned the need to bring out the practical application of subjects, in ways which would enhance rather than displace theoretical understanding. And, reflecting the now-familiar language of the GCSE criteria, he asked the committee to look at the extent to which A levels test knowledge, understanding, and skills, and the implications of the assessment procedures for teaching and learning. Finally he suggested that the committee would have to look both at the alternative provision for the 16–19 age-group that was provided by BTEC, CGLI, CVPE, and RSA (all that which is to come under the general control of the new National Council for Vocational Qualifications) and at the extent to which pupils who have followed GCSE courses may have become accustomed to a different kind of assessment procedure from that incorporated in A levels.

In this second document, then, the Secretary of State showed himself aware of some of the differing demands: breadth with no sacrifice of depth; practical content that will not displace the theoretical; the maintenance, even the raising, of 'standards', with a welcome none the less for those who might have approached learning and assessment in a new way.

The extent to which pupils at school progressing from the GCSE to A levels will find an unbridgeable gap will depend on the way in which 'differentiating' the curriculum and the assessment of pupils is interpreted in different schools, and for different courses. If, as seems probable, most teachers will sort out their pupils into the high and the low fliers at a fairly early stage, and if there is a whole separate set of papers in some subjects for the high and the low, then the difference between the higher grades of GCSE and O levels will not turn out to be very great. Despite all the detailed criteria set out for assessment, despite the emphasis on course-work, in the end 'high' GCSE will be familiar enough, and the transition to A level not a matter of genuine difficulty. As now, the decision who will proceed to A level, and thence to higher education will in effect have been taken at the end of the third year. Years 4, 5, 6, and 7 of school will, all of them, be directed towards the goal of higher education. The fears of the Scruton philosophy may well turn out to have been exaggerated.

Nevertheless it seems to me that this is a time when we have a chance to examine the utility of A levels in their present form, a chance that may have been missed by the terms of reference of the Higginson Committee. It is probably unrealistic to suggest that, so soon after the reorganizing and restructuring of examinations at 16 +, we can envisage yet another new system. Yet it is inevitable that at the present time of confusion and reform we ask why we should be dependent upon these two great blocks of examinations, at these two particular points in a student's school career.

GCE O and A levels were devised when a large proportion of children left school after the fifth year, and when it was therefore sensible to have a block of examinations taken in that year, to operate partly as a school-leaving certification, partly as a screen, to select those who would stay on. The 18 + examinations were seen, as the Secretary of State himself recognized, again partly as another such certificate for those who had stayed the next voluntary two years at school, partly as an aptitude test for those who were to go on to higher education, partly as a still more specific entry requirement for admission to specified courses in institutions of higher education. I have already argued the case for having public examinations of some kind for all pupils at school, for the benefit of the outside world. But I have yet to be convinced of the need that these should be taken at two particular times in a student's school career. Many fewer people leave school at 16 than did when the examinations were introduced; and more every year are being encouraged to stay at school or to leave only to go to sixth-form college, college of further education, or wherever else they may receive education that will lead to a higher accreditation. The case for a compulsory examination at 16+ seems increasingly weak (and the fact that such examinations are not mentioned in the Secretary of State's prospective for his newly invented Technology Colleges may reflect this). If we could be certain (as we ought) that every person of 16 had the opportunity to go on to further education or practical, examinable work, then we could drop the 16+ examination without loss, and with a possible simplification of the school curriculum up to that point.

But if that examination were dropped, would it not be all the more necessary to retain A levels, emphasizing their role both as school-leaving certificate and as entry test for higher education? I suspect that this may reflect the thought of the Secretary of State, in his insistence on retaining A levels as constituting a 'standard of excellence'. Moreover, I believe that he has another reason for clinging to the A level concept. The existence of A level courses may be seen not simply as a useful tool for individual pupils who may want to go further in their education (or have a certificate to show that they have not left school till they were 18); but as a measure of the standard of the school itself. A school that, though equipped with a sixth form, did not have good A level results could be picked out as an inefficient school. Schools (perhaps excluding the new Technology Colleges) should be judged according to *academic* criteria; and these could be supplied, as they always have been, by the size of the sixth form and the number of entries to universities—that is, by A level results. Only schools that satisfied such criteria would be judged 'value for money'.

But I believe it might be possible to get the universities and polytechnics in future to accept a way of selecting candidates that was radically different from either A levels alone, or A and AS levels. Universities and polytechnics, after all, are as much interested as anybody in what a student can do; and especially in what he understands. What he must be able to do is to learn new things. And in order for this to be possible, he must be able also to show that he understands what he has learned. A levels are notoriously less than perfect as a vehicle for showing this. Moreover, the Secretary of State has predicted that by the 1990s there will be proportionately more of the total population in higher education, whether at university or polytechnic. Some of these extra students will be people who are entering after several years in employment, or after years spent bringing up a family; others will be coming straight from secondary education. For both of these groups it will be convenient to have a method of selection that is both more flexible and more discriminating than A levels.

For everyone in higher education would agree that A levels are at best a very rough and ready guide to a pupil's future development. Often the most one can learn from them is that the student stuck out the course and actually learned enough to pass the examination, retaining what he learned long enough to get it down on paper. To know this much about a student is better than nothing. But it is not enough. One of the drawbacks of A level is that because it is an examination to be taken at a particular time, namely after two years of study in the sixth form (there are exceptions to this, but such is the general rule) it is taken by people who are at very different stages of development, of readiness for the examination, and, above all, of interest in the subject matter. Thus someone of mature judgement and sophisticated taste has to be taught and examined in literature alongside someone who has chosen that subject because it is thought to be relatively easy, has no aptitude for it nor any possible interest except in getting through the examination. The comments of Her Majesty's Inspectors on the teaching of A level English bear witness to this defect in the system. As far as the grades allotted to the candidates are concerned, a conscientious and uninterested student may very well do better than one who is imaginative and perhaps wayward. Neither in English literature nor in history are A level grades a good indicator of what is to come. In mathematics and the sciences they fail in a rather different way: they simply are not demanding enough, especially in mathematics. In universities with strong mathematics departments such as Cambridge and Warwick, no one would ever be admitted who had not achieved grade As in A level. But among those students a considerable number have great difficulty with the university course. They have simply not had the chance at school to demonstrate whether or not they are actually able to go on with mathematics. The same is true in the case of music. There is an enormous gap between what is required at school and what is required by at least some of the courses at university.

A levels, then, though relied upon at present as a higher education aptitude test, and regarded by many schools and many parents as a test of the academic respectability of schools themselves, are not wholly satisfactory for either of these purposes. It seems to me that we could learn to rely on a system that could both embrace a wider ability range and discriminate within it more accurately (both downwards and upwards) if we adopted the structure of graded tests. Moreover, such tests could be devised in such a way as to reflect what I have argued to be the most important feature of any new curriculum, the *equal* importance of the practical and the theoretical. It is for these two different reasons, then, that I advocate adopting graded tests. They would be more effective and useful; and at the same time they could be employed to reflect a new approach to the *balance* of education for which I have argued.

The various experiments taking place at the present time in the use of graded tests (for example in the Borough of Croydon) tend to show that this form of examination would, in all kinds of ways, be preferable to the system we have. But given the fact that the first GCSE examinations will have been held only in 1988, and that it would therefore be unrealistic to recommend their instant abandonment. And given also the Government's apparent determination to retain and strengthen A levels as a block of 18 + examinations, it is probably most useful to explore ways in which graded tests might be combined with both GCSE and

A level, at least as a beginning. The first step towards such a combination would be for universities and polytechnics to demonstrate their interest in using graded test results as either a part or the whole of entry qualifications. This would carry with it a responsibility on their part to help devise the tests, or at least to scrutinize their content. Indeed, this would be nothing new, since many tests devised by university departments of education are already the subject of research and development. The Oxford Examination Delegacy, for example, which has a strong university membership, has instituted an Oxford Certificate of Educational Achievement, consisting of three elements: the traditional examination element (GCSE or GCSE and A level); the graded-test element; and the school report or profile element. To introduce such a certificate nationwide would not be difficult, and would be almost certainly welcome to institutions of higher education.

Our knowledge of graded tests comes from modern languages, where tests have been in use for more than a decade;[8] from mathematics, where two sets of tests are currently in use; from science; and from the long-established Associated Board Examinations in music, dancing, and spoken English, or recitation. The modern-language tests were introduced specifically because teachers themselves were so keenly aware of the inadequacy of school modern-language teaching. It has in the past been notorious that a pupil in an English school, having learned French for seven years, and having even passed at grade A at A level, may yet be unable to utter more than a few halting sentences, and be hardly able to follow a simple conversation with a native speaker. Yet this same student may be quite good at translating from French to English or the other way round and may have a certain knowledge of the history of French literature and the critical points to be made about specified French texts. There could hardly be a better instance of the primacy of the written word compared with the spoken, of knowledge compared with skill.

Now it is true that, as we have seen, the GCSE is intended to test what a candidate can do as well as what he knows and understands; it is intended, therefore, that the oral part of the examination in

languages, including English, shall have a more central importance. Nevertheless the GCSE still labours under one tremendous
disadvantage. It has to be taken at one specific time, the end of the
fifth year. Even though the continuous assessment, course-work
elements will have been graded during the preceding two years, the
marks will be put together and the final grade awarded at this one
time. We have already noticed the difficulties involved in 'differentiating' the examination according to the presumed ability of
the candidates. But if within modern languages (to keep, for the
moment, to this example) a candidate for the GCSE were permitted to offer, as part of the evidence that went towards his certificate, the grades he had achieved in tests, starting from the most
elementary and progressing upwards according to his ability, the
'differentiation' problem would be virtually solved. For the
crucial characteristic of these tests is that they may be taken at any
time, according to the readiness of the student. Thus someone
who found learning a foreign language extremely difficult might
struggle to pass grade 1 spoken French by the time he was 16. His
pass at that grade would however show what he *could* do. On the
other hand a child who was brought up to be bilingual in French
and English or who had a natural facility for 'picking up'
languages could romp through his spoken French grades and have
reached the top by the time he was 16, while perhaps having
achieved lower grades both in written French and in other more
literary aspects of the subject. Once again differentiation would
not be a problem, and an accurate record of capability would be
gradually built up.

The best established model here is the Associated Board music
examination. The practical examinations have a syllabus that is
varied every year or two, but which, at each grade, represents a
consistent standard of difficulty. The rough guide is that there
should be approximately a year's progress-gap between each
grade. But there is no obligation to keep rigidly to this rule; nor
is it necessary to take examinations at all the grades. Many music
teachers who find that the examinations unduly restrict repertoire enter their students only for Grade VIII, the highest grade,
which is a minimum requirement for entry to music college.
Many candidates who start at the bottom skip grades on

the way up, or, perhaps because of pressure of other work, take more than a year between adjoining grades. Theory examinations exist alongside the practical examinations. At present they are perhaps somewhat mechanical and unimaginative. This is partly because most students take no theory examinations except Grade V, a required precondition for sitting O level music in the old days. The Grade V test was, therefore, taken by a number of students who had no particular interest in the theory of music, but who could be pushed through the test provided that they could learn the requirements and carry them out without too much in the way of understanding. There would be no difficulty in principle both in improving the theory tests and in extending both them and the practical tests so as to include, for example, score-reading and harmonization at the keyboard, aspects of the university courses in music which many students now find very difficult indeed. The Associated Board examinations, then, suitably extended, could well be used by universities and music colleges as the sole criterion by which students might be accepted to read music. A levels could quietly disappear. If this is possible, even easy, in the case of music, I see no reason why a similar pattern should not be established in other subjects, especially those where the feasibility of graded tests has already been established.

There are of course formidable difficulties to be overcome. In the first place it is essential to the concept of graded tests that they should be taken by students *when they are ready*, from time to time throughout their school career, or indeed after school (there is no reason why a grandmother and granddaughter should not practise side by side for their Grade I piano examination). This flexibility is an enormous advantage over one-off end-of-year examinations. But there are also difficulties. The whole concept of graded tests entails a belief in the idea of the 'readiness' of a student for a specific test, and the ability of the teacher to diagnose 'readiness' when he sees it. In the case of music examinations there are doubtless some teachers who keep their pupils back and refuse to enter them for an examination unless they are virtually certain that they will succeed. There are instrumental teachers who think only a distinction is worth considering and therefore may delay entering candidates, causing them to restrict their repertoire unduly. On the other hand there are teachers with low standards who think a mere pass at whatever grade is a feather in the cap, both of himself and of his pupil. Such teachers may enter too many pupils for examination. Nevertheless the idea of 'readiness' for a test must be one where the teacher has to be the ultimate judge; and this may lead to a certain amount of tension between parents and teachers.

There is a further difficulty. It is absolutely essential that each pupil's readiness for a particular grade should be judged individually. All the advantages would be lost if teachers decided, whether on grounds of convenience or of egalitarianism, that whole classes of students should be entered for a particular grade examination. It is true that this is likely to happen when a whole class has just embarked on a subject and may be thought ready to take Grade 1 all together. But it must never be forgotten that, if this happens, it happens by accident: it can be no part of the system that pupils should be entered for a test because of the age they are or the class they are part of. This is a fundamental principle.

The more this principle is understood and the more firmly it is adhered to, whether in practical or in theoretical subjects, the more difficult it will be for a school to organize its teaching. This is a fact that must be recognized by any teacher or any school who thinks seriously of embarking on graded tests as a means of supplementing, and perhaps ultimately supplanting, GCSE and A level examinations. If graded tests are widely adopted within a school and if they are used properly as a means of assessing individual pupils' ability and knowledge, according to their progress along the path of expertise, then the school must be prepared for classes that are grouped vertically, not horizontally. Though an individual pupil may be in his fourth-year class as far as the administration of the school goes, and as far as concerns his social activities or his out-of-school interests, the school must be prepared for him to go off and study the syllabus required for his graded tests alongside people who are not in his own year. Beginners' German may contain 11-year-olds and

17-year-olds (and, it is to be hoped, people who have long left school, and want to start a new language). Schools find it quite easy to adapt to this kind of grouping where they are dealing with 'marginal' subjects like music theory. When graded tests are used for subjects that are squarely part of the 'core curriculum', maths, sciences, languages, and English, there may be a certain reluctance to introduce such a system. But without it the advantages that a system of graded tests has over a GCSE or A level system will be lost.

The advantages of such vertical grouping are manifest. Teenage children, admitted by almost all teachers as the most difficult to teach, may become better motivated and better behaved if they have a short-term goal, passing the next grade on the ladder, and if they are working alongside people who are both older and younger than themselves. The crucial element in the system is that it should be modular. Each student can make up a package of tests to go for; he may repeat those that he fails, without the social disaster of being kept down a year; and he may make up a mix of practical and theoretical according to a plan worked out with his class teacher, and bearing in mind what he aims to do next. But no one should be permitted to leave school without at least some practical passes.

Needless to say, everything turns on the proper syllabus for each test being agreed, both in the practical and in the theoretical aspects of a subject. It then becomes a matter of supreme importance that teachers should be fair and exact in deeming their pupils 'ready' for a test; for it would be disastrous if a sense of failure were introduced again, by pupils being entered for tests they had no hope of passing. Equally, pupils who are very able should be allowed to forge ahead, to embark on tests beyond the scope of any so far envisaged. In this way boredom would be kept at bay; and universities might have some notion of the especial talents of some of their candidates. I believe that these conditions can be satisfied. The rearrangement of school classes might cause time-tabling difficulties at first (and might entail some classes being held after normal school hours, on Saturday mornings, or by arrangement in colleges of further education or neighbouring schools). Yet not only could such a rearrangement be brought about, with the will to do so, but it might come to be seen as greatly to the general advantage of the school.

The principle behind the system of graded tests is not dissimilar to that which has inspired the introduction of GCSE. The aim is to test children both in what they know and in what they can do. It is also to include *all* children in the system, excluding virtually none on grounds of ability. It seems to me that the graded-test system will simply carry out these functions more efficiently than the system of GCSE, followed by A levels or one of the range of non-school practical certificate tests.

Some teachers have objected to the scheme because, they say, it will not be clear what is to be included on the certificate. What, after a pass in Grade 1 practical electronics, is to be recorded as falling within the capacity of the child? How much detail will need to be recorded on the certificate about the criteria used to pass or fail the candidate; and how specific should be the description of the tasks he was set? I do not think these objections are very serious. The more frequently graded tests are used, the better will be the understanding of those who are to rely on them for the selection of candidates. Just as the certificates of the graded music examination now simply record a grade with a pass, merit, or distinction (further information can be acquired about the specific marks allotted to the student in each part of the examination), so, given time, a Grade 6 spoken German or a Grade 9 theoretical physics will speak for itself.

I hope that, in the end, such tests may replace *all* other examinations, making it unnecessary to hold any blocks of examinations at 16 + and at 18 + . In particular the block examination at 16 + appears to have lost its justification, when almost all 16-year-olds will go on to further education of some sort, whether in a sixth form or elsewhere. Graded tests would be far more informative for those involved in making up an individual programme fitted for each of those who is going on. However, it might be that, at first, such tests should be set only in those subjects which constitute the 'core curriculum' to be instituted nationally for all schools. To embark on such a common curriculum is a bold and, I believe, a necessary step on the part of government. It is the kind of good, intelligent paternalism that is urgently needed in our education system. But if, as is proposed, the core is to start to be taught from the primary schools, upwards, then it makes sense to introduce at the same time graded tests in each of the compulsory subjects, English, mathematics, modern languages, and science (the music examinations could hold their present place as optional). Thus children at their primary schools could be tested when they were ready, on the way up the school. The secondary school to which they went on would then have an accurate record of what they could do, and could save a great deal of time at present wasted in the transition from one school to another.

The Secretary of State has already proposed a set of tests to be used along with the national core curriculum. The idea of testing is, therefore, in some ways acceptable to the DES. Kenneth Baker's proposed tests, however, have a fatal drawback. They, like the GCSE and A level, are supposed to be taken at a particular age, at 7, 11, and 14. This is, as I have already argued, a recipe for disaster. No one who is either a parent or a teacher can fail to be aware of the vast differences between children of 7, not because of what they have been taught, but because of their rate of development and their maturity. I shall argue in the next chapter that it is part of a teacher's duties to attempt to redress the balance between children who have and those who have not the advantages of a supportive home. But even between children brought up in the same home with the same advantages, one with another, at 7 there are still huge differences. Some, because their interests lie elsewhere, may be barely able to read, and their writing may be rudimentary. Yet in the end they will catch up. Such differences, though they may be less marked when a child is 14, may yet be considerable. Is a child who fails a year test to be kept down? Will there not be some children who, though they may succeed in part of a test, or a test in a specific skill, may yet be unable ever to pass the whole of the test at every stage? However good our schools, there will emerge from them some people, quite capable of looking after themselves and of having a simple job, whose reading age will never be more than 8 or 9. Are these children yet again, as they were in the past, to be excluded from normal education?

We must insist on a system of tests that will be for the benefit of the pupils; that will test what each one can do in practical work and in theoretical understanding; and will serve as a motive for each to go on to the next stage. The only point of Mr Baker's tests that I can divine is that they will serve to check up on the teachers. The school will be monitored by means of the number of passes at 7, 11, and 14 that it can record. To ensure that teachers are teaching what they ought may be an admirable aim; but it must not be confused with a system of testing children. Pupils must not be used as a means to keep teachers up to the mark. Let us by all means have a national core curriculum; and let children be tested in the subjects that make up that curriculum. But let them advance along the road at their own pace, overcoming the obstacles on their way as best they can. Only so can we hope to retain their enthusiasm for what must inevitably sometimes seem a long and weary journey.*

* On 6 September 1987 there was a programme on London Weekend Television, produced by Glenwyn Benson, in which Peter Dines, Secretary of the Examination Council of London University, argued for the use of graded tests, to be linked with the GCSE, but replacing the element of 'final' 16+ examination. This programme appeared too late for me to refer to it in the foregoing chapter; but as far as I could see his scheme would satisfy practically all my demands.

The teaching profession

In 1978, when the Committee of Inquiry set up by the Government to consider special education published its report *Special Educational Needs*, they put at the top of their list of priorities the proper training of teachers. For they argued that no educational reforms of any sort could be implemented unless teachers were trained with these reforms in mind. Any educational idea could be put forward, and even generally accepted, but, however bright an idea it was, it would be guaranteed to die within a year or two unless it became a part of the presumptions lying behind the training of teachers. If this training is out of date or unimaginative or based on a discredited philosophy there is no hope for imaginative change within our schools. A way of thinking prevalent among those who train teachers takes a very long time indeed to work its way through the system. It was therefore of the greatest importance to change the attitudes of those engaged in the business of training. Such was the argument of the Committee of Inquiry in 1978; and it is an argument that is still valid today.

Moreover, if we are to believe, as we must, that education whether of children at school or of older students at polytechnics and universities is that upon which the status and the civilization of a country depends, then it is self-evident that those who actually provide education—not the planners nor the dispensers of funding but those who deliver whatever it is that pupils receive, the teachers themselves—are at the centre. We must learn to think of the teaching profession as a body of people on whom we can rely, whom we can trust, and on whom we place great responsibilities. This must be our attitude to all teachers, whether they teach in primary school, secondary school, or in establishments of further or higher education.

However, there is an important difference between school-teaching and teaching in colleges, universities and polytechnics; not a total difference in kind, but important none the less. Children go to school compulsorily, and at a formative age. The teacher at school is faced with pupils who *must* be there whether they like it or not; and if they do not like it, their whole future may be coloured by this fact. Though many students after school have to complete parts of their courses that they do not particularly enjoy and about which they may become relatively disaffected, yet nearly all of them are mature enough to understand that they may have to endure some tedium for the sake of their final goal. The goal is more or less visible to them, and they can understand their own responsibility in working towards it. Though the technique of teaching them is important, and though, as all undergraduates will testify, there is a great difference between good teachers and bad at university level, nevertheless the skills of teaching are less important for teachers at university or polytechnic level, simply because of the age, the intelligence, and the motivation of their pupils. When I discuss the training of teachers, then, I have in mind mainly those who will teach in school. But this should not be taken to mean either that I regard it as a matter of indifference whether or not those in polytechnics and universities are good teachers, nor that I regard school-teaching as something essentially different from teaching in tertiary education, still less that it is an inferior profession. Indeed, my assumption is that there is unity throughout the whole profession.

In the early 1970s there were about 40,000 people leaving college or university every year after training to be teachers. There were 180 institutions, not counting 27 university departments, that provided training. By 1983 the number of students leaving training each year had dropped to under 16,000 and the number of training institutions had declined to 53, the university departments still numbering 27. Many of the training institutions (colleges of higher education, as they are often called) have now diversified so as to offer degree and diploma courses other than those directly related to teaching. They were obliged to do this, if they were to stay open as the numbers of teachers in training declined. But it has to be said that the academic standards in some of these colleges are not at all high, even though they award degrees validated either by the Council for National Academic Awards (CNAA) or a local university. The low academic standing of these colleges is one aspect of the training of teachers that gives cause for concern.

The Department of Education and Science has always kept a strict watch over the numbers of teachers in training, attempting to forecast the numbers needed in the light of the projected school population in future years. These projections and forecasts have not always been particularly accurate; moreover there has often appeared to be so much concern with the numbers of teachers to be trained that the content of the training, its effectiveness, and its standing in the hierarchy of higher education in general have been forgotten. At any rate, at the present time, though there are far fewer teachers in training than there were ten or fifteen years ago, a higher proportion of these are being trained to teach in primary schools, and the general academic reputation of teacher training is low.

Ever since the publication of the James Report in 1972 (*Education: a framework for expansion*), there has been a steady increase in the proportion of those entering the teaching profession who are honours graduates. When the degree of B.Ed. was first introduced, there was a choice between a three-year ordinary degree course and a four-year honours degree. Now the ordinary degree has more or less disappeared. Most primary school teachers take the four-year course and end with a B.Ed. (Hons.). Most secondary school teachers take a university or polytechnic degree in a subject of their choice, and then do a year's training ending with a Postgraduate Certificate of Education (PGCE) taken in a university, polytechnic, or, occasionally, a college of higher education (a small number of secondary teachers do a B.Ed., but this is the exception). There is an increasing number of university students who choose to teach in primary schools, and so the number of PGCE courses directed towards primary teaching is gradually increasing. Thus the declared aim of the Government following the James Report, to make teaching an 'all-graduate' profession, has by now been virtually realized, though the level of the degree varies greatly.

It would be satisfactory if one could infer that the status of the profession was rising in society as a whole as the number of graduate teachers increases. But that is far from the case. Indeed the opposite appears to be true. It is the purpose of this chapter to examine the causes of the low standing of teachers and to suggest ways in which their position could be improved. For as long as teachers are not regarded as true professionals, upholding their own professional standards, and to be relied on for their specialist expertise, we shall not have an education system that we can believe in either. It is easy, at the time of writing, to point to the disruption of school education by the long-drawn-out industrial action on the part of teachers (1985–7) and to say, 'How could such teachers be regarded as proper professionals, since they are prepared to sacrifice the good of their pupils in so flagrant a manner?' And there is no doubt that the 1980s will go down in educational history as one of the most disastrous times in the relation between the teaching profession and the public. Nevertheless it would be absurd to pretend that the troubles of the 1980s were the *cause* of the low regard in which teachers have been generally held. The industrial action was the outcome of a long story of underpayment, and especially undervaluing, of teachers. The notorious 'Removal of Negotiating Rights' in 1986, when the pay dispute and the dispute about contractual obligations were settled by the direct intervention of Kenneth Baker, was a culmination and a symbol, in the eyes of the teachers, of the downgrading of their place in society. The strikes in many ways made things worse; but things were bad to start with.

The more frantically government, any government, tries to improve educational provision, the more manifest it becomes that, in the end, innovation and improvement can come about only through the agency of teachers. An education is no better than the teachers who implement it. If teachers are to be good, they must be believed to be so; and their training must form the basis of that belief.

This ought not to need saying. For who would doubt that a doctor needs to be properly trained if he is to be trusted, or an accountant, a solicitor, or an estate agent? Individuals within all these professions may be good or bad at their job, may be morally respectable or disreputable in a professional context. But the profession as a whole of which they are members is reputable, self-disciplined, and a proper object of public faith. Why is the same not true of teachers? One part of the answer is that there are still those who think that the training of teachers is unnecessary, at best an attempt to make respectable something which is not, and cannot be, respected, namely the science of education itself. For example the Hillgate Group's radical manifesto *Whose Schools?* contains the following recommendation:

Schools should be free to employ graduates directly on leaving university. The present system obliges potential teachers to spend a year working for the largely worthless Graduate Certificate of Education . . . a practice which discriminates heavily against those who have had the benefit of a university education, by placing an obstacle between them and the classroom.[1]

In the body of the text they write:

Teaching, like business, is a form of practical knowledge and may be as much destroyed as enhanced by the attempt to impart it as a theoretical discipline . . . We should like to see 'educationists' . . . deprived of authority, either to train teachers or to impose their counsels on the classroom. Such people, we believe, should be confined to the university and polytechnic departments whose disciplines they claim to apply . . . We also believe that the present system of 'in-service' training for teachers is insidious, giving spurious credentials to those who least deserve them, and discriminating heavily against those teachers whose main interest, competence and labour are spent in the teaching of children.[2]

The authors of these words plainly have no direct experience of teaching in schools as they are today, and are without either interest in or sympathy for the complex problems which are involved. They are perhaps to some extent victims of the myth of the 'born teacher', a myth that particularly endears itself to middle-aged persons looking back on their own school days. I do not for one moment deny that some teachers are naturally better at teaching than others, or that to some the skills and tricks of teaching come easily, to others with more difficulty. The same, after all, is true of actors or riders or musicians. But even the born teacher must be taught a number of aspects of his work: what sort of records he must keep; how to judge the progress or lack of progress of individual pupils in his class; how to encourage parental co-operation; how to set and mark new-style examinations; how to respond to abuse from pupils. There are innumerable areas, apart from the academic development of his own subject, where a teacher needs to be introduced to a proper professional approach to his task. The untrained scholar straight from university, filled with the love of his subject and longing to impart the same enthusiasm to his keen young pupils, may do very well, if he is lucky, in a small selective school. But he is not likely to make much of a success of more adventurous teaching. If the value of training for membership of a profession is denied, the profession itself is downgraded, since there can be no other way of introducing and insisting upon standards of performance, uniform as far as possible among all teachers, except through their training.

Alongside the attack on training itself, there is a different, though related, attack to which teachers are often subjected. According to this view, teachers do not need to be trained nor to be especially respected, because, it is said, teaching is easy. Primary school teachers are particularly criticized for pretending to be professional, when, in fact, all they do is to purvey wares that we all have in abundance. We all know how to read and write and calculate: if we had time, we could all teach these skills to our children. Primary school teachers know nothing that we don't know. Anyone could do their job. It's 'a doddle', and so it has been described. As for secondary school teachers (and teachers in sixth-form colleges and colleges of further education), even if they may be allowed to be experts as far as concerns their academic subjects, still their life is easy, so it is alleged, because they work such short hours, and have such long holidays.

This attack is perhaps the most common, and the most ignorant of all. No teacher, whatever the age of the children he teaches, works short hours. After school is over there is work to correct, lessons to prepare, professional meetings to attend (to say nothing of the kinds of work still undertaken by many teachers, like making costumes for the school play, transcribing music for the brass ensemble, and singing in the school choir). The holidays are neither particularly long nor can they be all holiday. It is only out of term that a teacher has time to keep up with his subject, think about a new syllabus, prepare not just one lesson at a time but a whole coherent course of lessons. If a serious teacher were to total up his hours of work during the year, he would turn out to be as hard-pressed as any 9-to-5 office worker.

In a way these forms of attack are similar. Whether a critic openly says that teaching is easy or whether, relying on the myth of the Born Teacher, he says that a teacher does not need training (indeed that training is a fraud on the public), in either case he is downgrading the teacher. We keep our respect for those who have jobs we acknowledge we could not do ourselves, whose expertise is mysterious and obviously slow to be acquired.

In England (though less in Scotland, and hardly at all in other European countries) the schoolteacher has always been despised. A 'schoolmistress' used to be despised because she was, typically, a spinster, and therefore thought to have a limited experience and a distorted view of life. A schoolmaster, though perhaps a less obvious target, was nevertheless looked down on simply because he worked among children and took school seriously, school being a topic not worthy of the consideration of a fully adult, sophisticated man. Such attitudes have a long history, and they are difficult to eradicate. No wonder, then, that when teachers try to turn themselves into acknowledged professionals they are often still decried. They cannot succeed in laying the veneer of 'trained professional' on a person so long looked down on. After all, we have all been to school, and, mercifully, outgrown it. From the point of view of the successful business man or politician, the sophisticated journalist or fashion-writer, school is something we would prefer to forget. Even if we have children who are at school, we can afford to take school life with a pinch of salt. We can afford to be detached, patronizing, and only occasionally interested. This is what lies behind the attitude of much of society towards teachers. It is an attitude seldom articulated, but entrenched for all that. If education as a whole is to improve we must somehow change it.

There are at least two other sources of the low repute of teachers at the present time. First, and most obviously, teachers seem to have demeaned themselves by their industrial action. While on the one hand regarding teaching as a somewhat lowly job, on the other hand there is no doubt that society thinks of teachers as people who ought not to behave like other workers and go on strike for better pay and conditions. By so doing they have put themselves into the category of manual workers, essentially unionized. When they actually begin to describe themselves as an industrial work-force within which 'blue-collar' is lined up against 'white-collar' then the last shreds of respect may be withdrawn from them. I quote from a speech made at a conference of the National Association of Head Teachers in 1987 by a northern headmaster. He complained that the teachers on strike had succeeded in depressing the salaries of headteachers like himself, because it was they, the class teachers, who had dominated the pay talks. 'What other industry', he asked, 'has blue-collar workers negotiating for white-collar workers and management?'[3] He may have meant this as a joke; but it was a joke that would chill the blood of many people who would like to think of teachers as totally different from workers in industry, whatever the colour of their collar. If what this headmaster was calling for was a proper system of pay differentials within the teaching profession, rather than a uniform increase for all teachers, then he doubtless had right on his side. But the language he used to make this claim was designed to alienate the public, and cause them to place teachers ever lower in the social hierarchy.

It might be argued that we ought not to think in terms of a social hierarchy. But, like it or not, our society is stratified and we are all more or less, and in different ways, snobbish. It is not in the interests of education as a whole that teachers should be seen as belonging at the bottom of the pile. Professor Brian Holmes, writing in *Education Today* in summer 1987, put the point thus: 'The difference between a Union and a Profession is that the former views the interests of its members as paramount; members of a profession are as much concerned about the interests of their clients as . . . about their own interests. The crux of this analysis is that . . . teachers do not now meet professional requirements.' Of course this is an over-simple way to state the case. Even though doctors do not regard the British Medical Association as a trade union, still it is often hard to believe that doctors are *as much* interested in their clients, the patients, as in their own means of making money. And the same could be said of lawyers or accountants. Nevertheless there is truth in what Brian Holmes says and many people would agree with him.

Another factor of a different kind prevents the general public from respecting teachers as professionals. Besides being increasingly unionized, teachers are also thought to have become increasingly politicized, especially teachers in London and the inner cities. It is very hard to judge the accuracy of this sort of accusation against teachers. Certainly the Local Authorities, up till now their employers, and the Inner London Education Authority in particular, are highly political, and this was the basis of the Conservative determination to diminish the powers of Local Authorities to vanishing point. It is certainly true, as well, that many parents fear that their children are being indoctrinated at school with political views which they, the parents, do not share. And even if they do share them, they may well feel that teachers ought not to try to get their pupils to adopt any political views at all, left-wing or right. Teaching, it is felt, ought to be distinguished from indoctrination or propaganda.

There is a fine distinction to be drawn here which I suspect cannot be drawn once and for all, or by means of the rigid application of criteria. If it is desirable, as most people think that it is, for children to be taught to be honest, kind, generous, truthful, and fair—to be given, that is, moral education—why should it be thought wrong for them to be taught the evils of exploitation, greed, or aggression on a political scale? For this is what the 'political' teachers would claim that they were doing. And they would further claim that issues such as pacificism, or anti-nuclear policies or the defence of homosexualism were all moral issues, though with a political dimension. They would indeed refuse to recognize a difference between the moral and the political. And yet many people would hold that politically motivated teachers, determined to inculcate their own political principles, were betraying their profession. Morals are all right;

political convictions are another thing. Political teachers are not, in short, teaching but indoctrinating their pupils.

More than twenty years ago, much of the writing in the philosophy of education was concerned to try to draw the distinction between educating and indoctrinating. In the work of R. S. Peters, the founding father of modern educational philosophy, this was a recurrent theme. For example, in *Education and Ethics* he wrote:

What matters is not what any individual thinks, but what is true. A teacher who does not equip his pupils with the rudimentary tools to discover this is substituting indoctrination for teaching. Paradoxically enough a teacher must both be an authority, and teach in such a way that pupils become capable of showing him where he is wrong. The teacher is an agent of change and challenge . . . this is tantamount to maintaining that the business of the teacher is to teach . . . not to indoctrinate. Teaching involves the passing on of skills, knowledge or modes of conduct in such a way that the learner is brought to understand and evaluate the underlying rationale for what is presented to him. Indoctrination, on the other hand, involves either the mere inculcation of beliefs or the addition of a rationale which discourages the evaluation of beliefs, e.g. the appeal to authority as a backing.[4]

We may sympathize with Peters's desire to draw a distinction between the legitimate influence of a teacher, educating his pupils to think independently and pursue the truth, and on the other hand the domination of the propagandist, unduly influencing his pupils to believe what he believes; but the suggestion, contained in this passage, that the distinction can be drawn by calling on the difference between a proper and a fake rationale is unduly optimistic. It stems from a time when moral and political philosophy were firmly founded on utilitarianism. If you could show someone that his behaviour, private or public, caused more harm than benefit, then you had shown him the underlying rationale for giving up such behaviour forthwith. Being rational was being able to calculate the harms and benefits that flowed from liberalism as opposed to fascism, from tolerance as opposed to prejudice, from racial openness as opposed to exclusiveness. Twenty years on, such a moral philosophy seems naïve. It rests on an assumption that consensus exists, if only we pause long enough to locate it, and on a general preference for reason rather than passion which few would be confident of finding in society today. But if there is no consensus, if reason is not generally thought of as the best or only suitable tool with which to shape and govern either our personal lives or the world, how are we to distinguish indoctrination from education? How are we to justify the feeling we may have that some teachers are exploiting their position by politicizing the class-room, and making it little better than a platform for unargued, even dangerous, views?

There are two things to be said. First, Peters is partly right: a good teacher is *fair*; and that means not only being fair to his pupils but to people outside the class-room who may not share his views. A teacher who goes into the class-room knowing that what he intends is to win converts is betraying his obligation of fairness. He must allow, and let his pupils see that he allows, a view other than his own. For in the realm of politics it is not a matter of his presenting 'the truth': he is, and must recognize that he is, presenting one side of a dialogue. He need not conceal his own views; but he must clearly mark to his pupils that these are indeed opinions, not facts.

Secondly, it is important (however difficult) to distinguish the political from the moral; and this may be done in terms of the scope of the imperatives contained in each. We do not want teachers who say, 'In my view (but it is only an opinion) you should not bully a child who is young and helpless.' We want a teacher who will unequivocally say 'bullying is wrong' or even, in the heat of the moment, '*Stop* what you are doing,' and 'Never let me catch you doing that again.' In this way a moral injunction is, and ought to be, different from a political injunction. A teacher may say, in effect, 'I am a Labour voter.' But he must imply 'It is for you, when the time comes, to make up your own mind.' For to be Left or Right in politics is to take on a perfectly general commitment to one or other standpoint, whichever seems on balance to be better (and 'better' may, of course, include 'morally better'). A child at school has no power as yet to act politically; he can at best begin to survey the scene and see how he will act in future. The scope of morality on the other hand is, even for a child, the here-and-now. Morally, but not politically, a child is *tempted*; he has to be taught to curb his selfishness, his anger, his greed. He has to be taught, in the immediate environment of the class-room and the playground, to recognize that there are other people who matter besides himself. School is for most children the place where they first become aware of a moral dimension to life, of the existence of other people of equal importance with themselves. A teacher who does not realize this, and who does not impose proper respect for others *here and now* is failing in his educative duty. The difference between this sort of education and political propaganda is enormous. A child has no immediate concern with politics, only an indirect or academic concern. With morality he is intimately concerned from the beginning. He has to learn to behave well. And about what counts, within the limited context of school, as good behaviour there *is* consensus. We all approve of truthfulness, kindness, and courage; we all disapprove of dishonesty, cruelty, and cowardice. The human virtues, at this domestic level, are not really in dispute. It is not therefore really necessary to agonize at a theoretical level about how to distinguish political indoctrination from moral education. It is not to be desired or expected that teachers should refuse to discuss issues such as racism, feminism, pacifism, homosexuality, or nuclear power. But they can discuss them as problematic, complex matters, on which evidence must be weighed up before judgements are made and on which conclusions may legitimately differ. Without concealing their own views, they should still make it clear that there are others who interpret the world differently, and that their pupils must learn to make their own properly based judgements. Parents will not respect or trust teachers until they are convinced that teachers themselves can somehow draw the distinction between the moral and the political and, abandoning dogmatic politics, pursue the moral with vigour.

So what is to be done? How are teachers to gain, or regain, the respect of parents and the public at large? For if they are not respected, then education itself will not be properly valued. In the 1940s education was thought to be the great good which, along with health services, must be distributed fairly to everyone in the new and newly egalitarian post-war society. Nearly fifty years later we see a kind of split: education is thought of as valuable, if at all, mainly on the grounds that it leads to jobs, and through jobs to possible prosperity. The earning capacity of ex-pupils is a criterion of worth in both schools and universities. But teachers are on the whole despised and underpaid. Grandiose new ideas have been forthcoming about the new kind of schools and the new kind of examinations that provide a new and better kind of education. But nothing much has been said about how a new kind of teacher is to be found who will man the schools and provide the education that is desired. After all, if education is nothing but a way to affluence, we should not be surprised if students in universities and polytechnics can think of a quicker, more direct route than becoming teachers. To become affluent themselves and encourage the wealth-producing potential of others, they will not go into the class-room, but into the city. Somehow the universities, the ultimate source of educational 'standards', have got to show that they, at least, believe in education, and therefore in teachers.

The answer to this problem cannot lie in the abandonment of the training of teachers. On the contrary, it must lie in a new kind of training, a training that will turn teachers into a body of professionals who can take charge of the education they provide, can impose their own professional standards on the methods of provision, and speak with the voice of authority on what it is that children need who are to be educated, recognizing the genuine power they have to shape the future. It is time to consider the nature of such training.

First we must ask what should be the content of training. We can then go on to think about how training should be organized if it is to be effective. For the most conspicuous and disastrous fact about the education of children at the present time is its wastefulness. Every year hundreds of children leave school without having gained any permanent benefit from the years they have spent there. The teachers of these children have been wasting their time, and we have all been wasting our money. There is a vast gap between successful and unsuccessful school education; and this is the gap that must be bridged. If the comprehensive ideal were to be abandoned we should, in my view, be admitting defeat. We should be acknowledging that the bridge could never be built between success and failure. And so the training of teachers must address itself specifically to this problem: how are we to provide a body of people committed to teaching in such a way that *all* children profit from their time at school?

The first goal for any training course must be that those who undertake it should be given the faith and the confidence that such teaching is possible. They must come to believe that they are capable of teaching anyone, not just the bright and the keen, but those who are reluctant and unapproachable, and for whom the school curriculum seems remote. I am not suggesting that the training of teachers should concentrate on nothing but how to teach alienated, underprivileged, disaffected pupils. It is rather that the idea of teaching itself, helping children, enabling them to become interested and competent, should be given priority over everything else. The training of teachers has never really caught up with the 1944 Education Act, still less with the growth of comprehensive schools. The best teachers will still be enthusiastic about their own subjects, and anxious to share their enthusiasm. Such has always been a characteristic of a good, and indeed of a 'born' teacher. But this is not enough. It is not this aspect of his work for which a teacher needs to be trained. He needs training to enable him to use his enthusiasm to best effect for the benefit of all, or any, of his potential pupils.

We have to recognize that teaching is a practical activity and the first need a trainee has is to learn the practical techniques of managing a class. He must learn, not primarily by exhortation, but by observation and practice, how to distinguish pupils within a class according to their needs; and must be taught how to hold together at one and the same time the idea of the class as a crowd or group, and that of the class as a collection of individuals. As a crowd a class may have a life and character of its own, and may be powerful, threatening, or potentially destructive. It is over the class as a crowd that the teacher has to learn to establish his own personal authority, just as an actor must over an audience. With confidence, a teacher may come to

love the sense of power he has over a class. Again the analogy
with the actor is illuminating. To feel that he is able to change
the mood of a class, to relax control, knowing that he can pull
in the reins at any time, that he can amuse, inspire, sympathize,
threaten—this is a great and appropriate reward for a teacher
who is successful. Such pleasure in power is not evil or corrupt,
it is simply one of the proper pleasures that result from competence. But a trainee teacher cannot learn to experience it
without the help and co-operation of a good school in which to
practise. I shall return to this requirement in a moment.

In so far as the class is made up of individuals, once again the
trainee teacher needs to be taught what his relationship with
these individuals should be, and what his duties are towards
them. Some of these lessons are relatively straightforward. He
must learn, for example, how to keep proper records of
individual achievement and progress; he must recognize it as a
duty to pay no more attention to one member of the class than
another (easy enough to say, but hard to achieve); he must treat
everybody with equal courtesy and consideration, and show no
signs of favouritism or the opposite; he must watch himself for
signs of racial or gender discrimination. He must undertake
always to correct and return homework within reasonable time.
Under the new system of examination, as will be clear from the
last chapter, he must learn the art of continuous assessment, and
the setting and grading of projects that will form parts of the
final grade.

There are more difficult aspects of the teacher's relation to his
pupils which must also be taught and discussed as an essential
part of training; the aspects I refer to are largely a matter of
judgement and tact, and may therefore be difficult both to teach
and to learn. They fall within the confused and problematic area
of the relation of teachers to pupils through parents. If teachers
are to regard themselves, and be regarded by others, as truly
professional, what attitude should they adopt to the parents of
their pupils? If a parent is to take a teacher seriously and trust
his professional judgement, then the relationship between them
must be of its own kind, specific to education. It is of no use for
a teacher to borrow a professional relationship from elsewhere,

from the world of doctors, social workers, or police. In particular, teachers need to distinguish themselves from social workers, overlapping though their responsibilities may often seem to be. This does not mean that teachers should not collaborate with social workers. Far from it. But they must work together with integrity, holding fast to their own values, and arguing for the good of their pupil/client from their own standpoint. In 1987 two of the teachers' unions called for a kind of social-work training for teachers, specifically to help them to identify at school those children who were being subjected to abuse or neglect at home. The aim is admirable, and it is true that teachers are in a good position to detect such children. Nevertheless the roles of teacher and the social worker must be kept distinct.

For a social worker is essentially non-judgemental, and must try to be so. At first sight this might seem to be a condition to which the teacher should also aspire. The concept of the Neutral Teacher was one that had a certain vogue in the 1960s and 1970s, and there was considerable debate among educational philosophers about what his neutrality should consist in and how he should preserve it. But a teacher cannot, in fact, be expected to adopt and maintain an Olympian stand, observing calmly the goings on in his class-room. Even if, as we have seen, he has to try to teach his pupils to look all round a particular question, on the political front, without prejudging for them any answers, yet in the field of instant morality he must be resolute, strong, and, if necessary, interventionist. There is no case at all for a *morally* neutral teacher; he must be seen by his pupils, whatever their age, to be on the side of fairness, honesty, and kindness. He cannot be non-judgemental because he is in the judgement seat for most of his working life, especially when his pupils are young, hardly out of the nursery.

Moreover if he, the teacher, comes to think about it (which he may never do) he will see that the theory that lies behind the social worker's attitude to his clients is different from that which, albeit obscurely, lies behind his own. Social workers tend towards the belief that people are the product of their environment, emerging to behave as they do as a result of their circumstances rather than of their choice. A social worker's client is a part of a whole community which itself is part of a wider social order. A child, for a social worker, is part of a family; a family itself is part of a social setting not of its own making. It is difficult for a social worker to think of people one at a time. His 'case load' consists, at the very least, of a number of 'family units'. Though a social worker may in fact see his client by himself more often than a teacher sees his pupil, yet he will always be trying to relate this client to his wider ambience; and where a client is in trouble, has fallen behind with his rent, is homeless, doesn't know how to apply for the benefits he is entitled to, then the social worker must try to organize his circumstances so that these problems no longer arise. He is not committed to trying in any way to change the client himself. In fact he doubtless regards that as impossible. The teacher, on the other hand, must be, professionally speaking, an individualist. First and foremost his concern must be with each child in his class, as an individual potential learner. Professionally, he is committed to optimism: he must believe it possible that the child himself will change. And this amounts to saying that the teacher, unlike the social worker, must, whether he has ever thought about it or not, believe in free-will. A child—or anyone—*can*, if he decides to, change himself. A teacher seeks not to change the circumstances that make up the world of a particular child, but to open up a new world to be explored. A child is not doomed by his environment; on the contrary he can be made to believe that, if he tries, he can break away from it, either actually or through his imagination. The old cliché written by teachers since time immemorial on their reports that 'John could do better', irritating as it may be for parents to read, nevertheless encapsulates the teachers' philosophy. He *could* do better if he tried; and he *can* try. There is no such thing as a child for whom there is no hope.

When a teacher first encounters a child, he should be able to put out of his mind anything he may know about him: who his parents are, how much of a nuisance his older sister was, that he is on probation, that he is black or a Jew. The professional teacher must as far as possible strive to regard his pupil as a person in his own right, a *tabula rasa*, someone who, being human, has the capacity to learn to 'do better'. The teacher must always be ready to be surprised. He should never say to himself, 'This is a child from a broken home: expect trouble'; nor 'This is a professor's daughter: she will be quick to learn; and, if not, it's laziness'; nor 'Here's a West Indian: not much hope here'; nor 'Here's a girl; no hope of a good grade in physics.' All these presuppositions must be laid aside, and will be by the professional teacher. The essential optimism involved in the very process of teaching consists in ignorance: ignorance of what a pupil may turn out to be able to do, how far he may go. I am not saying that a teacher should literally be kept in ignorance of his pupil's social circumstances. There may well be cases where he will need to bear these in mind, if he is to be fair to the child. It is rather that a teacher who is a professional, and professionally trained, will be able, despite the knowledge he may have, to regard his pupil as a free agent not wholly determined by his genes or his circumstances, but able, if inspired to do so, to make an effort and to improve.

The difference between teachers and social workers in this respect has consequences for the proper role of the teacher *vis-à-vis* the parents of his pupils. The professional relationship of the teacher must be first and foremost with the child, not with his parents. The child coming to school, even if he is only four or five years old, is being offered a new chance; a chance to start again, and be a different person. He is no longer bound by the chains of his circumstances or his family. And this is just as much true of a child from an affluent or intellectual home as for one from a deprived or impoverished background. At school all equally have a chance to experiment and try out a new world. This is the essential function of school.

It might seem to follow from this that a teacher must keep the parents of his pupils at arm's length, in case he develops a relationship with the parent instead of with the child, who should be his primary concern. To a certain extent I believe that this is true. At all costs a teacher must not be seen to gang up against the child with the parents in cases of conflict. Nor must he always accept uncritically a parent's view of what is best for a child. Herein lies one of the dangers of assuming that parents are the right people to exercise power in a school, to determine the curriculum, to decide what is the best method of teaching or who is to be hired or fired.

As part of the general aim of stripping Local Authorities of power (and perhaps also of putting recalcitrant teachers in their place) it became a central item in Tory education policy in the late 1980s to promote the power of parents. As long ago as 1977 there was a move (in, for instance, the Taylor Committee Report) to involve parents more in the governing of schools. And since then parents have increasingly been spoken of as those who should have ultimate authority to decide whether a school should or should not seek independence from Local Authority power; to decide whether or not a school should be selective or comprehensive; to determine, by the exercise of choice of where to send their children, which schools being 'popular' should flourish, which should wither away. But it should be remembered that a school is not a club or society of adults, to be run by its keener members. It is an educational institution for children, with a life and ethos of its own, with a history, and a future that will far outlive the somewhat ephemeral interest in it of any individual parent, who tends to be concerned with the school only while his children are of school age. An educational body must make its own policies and set its own standards, not, it is true, without regard to the wishes of parents, but certainly not subject to parental whim. It is sometimes thought that parent power will prevent a school curriculum, or a school ethos, from becoming too political. But parents are also political, as much liable as teachers to wage party warfare. And, more than teachers, parents are liable to take into account only one aspect of the school, that which most immediately affects their own child. If they are to take a part in governing a school, they must be brought to realize the requirements of the *whole* school, as an institution.

A school, essentially, consists of pupils and their teachers. So if parents have criticisms of individual members of staff, they must not feel that they have a right to approach the particular individual teacher with complaints. They must always seek to discuss their complaints with the head, who is head of the school *as a whole*. Schools must not be run on the lines of a consumer-orientated service, like a hotel or restaurant. In one sense the parent is a consumer, and may hope to exercise the choice and influence that the market-place consumer may exercise on the provision of his needs. But, in a much more important sense, it is the child, not his parents, who is the consumer. It is for his sake that the institution exists, and it is he, not his parents, who must flourish if the school is to be deemed a success. It is on these grounds that teachers must take an independent and professional stand, prepared, if necessary, to defy a parent for the sake of what they believe is the good of the child.

I have already called attention to the fact that parents are not always conspicuously keen to take part in the government and regulation of schools. It was a part of the 1986 Education Act to lay down that every school should hold at least one parent meeting each year, at which decisions affecting the school could be taken. Many schools found that the number of parents attending such meetings was in single figures—and that the meetings were seldom quorate. Small wonder that teachers were sceptical and felt that parents did not take school seriously.[5]

On the other hand a teacher must not so far distance himself from the parents that he seems to regard their views as worth nothing. He must not adopt the god-like stance of an old-fashioned doctor who can issue 'doctor's orders' and expect them to be obeyed. It seems to me that a teacher's professional role is to let his own realistic optimism about a pupil (based as it must be on a knowledge of what the child as a separate individual can do and what he wants to do) spill over so that it affects the parents as well. Parents must be encouraged by teachers themselves to be optimistic and open-minded, ready to be surprised and impressed by their own child, even if he does not turn out exactly as they would have hoped or forecast. Not only will the growth of such an attitude in parents towards their children be very much in the best interests of the children, but it will also engender a parental trust in the teacher, a liking and respect for him, that will have beneficial consequences for education as a whole.

To cause parents to feel this kind of hope for their children, and the associated trust in their school, the most important requirement for a teacher is that he should be *confident*. He must be able to argue in favour of what he is teaching and the way he is teaching it. A teacher cannot adopt a proper attitude towards parents, or achieve a balance between asserting his own views and listening to theirs, if he is himself unsure of what he is doing or why he is doing it. Neither can he exercise authority if he is hesitant, disillusioned, or resentful. We are accustomed to thinking in terms of the authority that teachers must exercise over their pupils. It is just as important that they should be authoritative in their contacts with parents. For this is what conscious expertise and professionalism entails. And so we may return to the necessity of training. It may be that an old and experienced teacher could find in himself this kind of authority, arising from long experience and accumulated expertise. But a young teacher, who has just as much need of authority, if not more, can acquire it only through thorough and wholly practical training.

Though it is true that, within the last decade, teacher training has changed and improved to a considerable extent, there is still a long way to go. In 1987 the DES published a survey of initial teacher training in the public sector (that is, in institutions other than university departments of educational studies) between 1983 and 1985.[6] As is usual in such reports there was a good deal of blandly appreciative comment; but still there were some damning criticisms. And it has to be remembered that in the universities, not covered by the report, the standards of practical preparation of teachers may have been just as low as those in the public sector, if not lower; and over 60 per cent of all secondary teachers who are trained work for their postgraduate certificates of education in university departments.

Taking the training of primary school teachers first, the main criticisms contained in the report were that those responsible for training had mostly taught only in secondary schools, and had little experience of primary school teaching. In the case of students reading for the degree of B.Ed. it was found that even where the academic standards required of students in their specialist subjects were adequate (and these cases were not numerous) there was a quite inadequate attempt to relate those subjects to actual teaching. Much of the four-year course had really nothing to do with education at all, but was devoted to sub-university-level courses in English, music, mathematics, or whichever might be the student's chosen subject: 'In most instances the amount of time students spent on specialist study was insufficient to provide them with adequate knowledge and confidence in a particular area of the primary curriculum.' And, in addition, the inspectors went on,

It was a matter of concern that so few B.Ed. degrees contained a *method course* designed for students to consider the application of their specialist subject to children's learning. As one of the potential strengths of the B.Ed. is the opportunity it offers for linking the students' specialism to their professional training, this is a disappointing and serious weakness.[7]

Very much the same criticisms were levelled against those PGCE courses that were designed to train graduates for teaching in primary schools, and in these the constraint of time (the whole professional training having to be fitted into, at most, thirty-six weeks) was in itself an extra obstacle. The inspectors wrote, 'The difficulties of achieving both academic credibility and professional relevance within the same course were all too often evidenced.'

Turning now to secondary school teaching, on the whole the inspectors' reservations about current training were even more marked. Once again they noticed a failure to train teachers to relate their specialist subjects to the needs of the class-room. They also noticed a general lack of training in the relating of a particular subject specialization to the curriculum as a whole. They expressed themselves seriously concerned by the lack of attention to the problems of differing pupil needs:

Fewer than half the PGCE and B.Ed. subject method courses were providing students with an understanding of the varieties of pupils' needs in terms of ability, culture and background, or helping students to make the teaching of their subject relevant and interesting to a full range of pupils; in only a few of these cases was this preparation of a high standard. In the others, students were not being adequately helped to recognise that the content and processes of learning have to be appropriate to the pupils' level of understanding and previous experience, that they benefit from approaching new ideas through a familiar context, and that they need to appreciate the relevance of what they are learning to their immediate or future needs.[8]

Of course, as we saw in Chapter 2, the 'born teacher', or the teacher of common sense, will grasp at once that in order to capture his audience he must make what he says funny, appealing, or pertinent. But there may be many trainee teachers to whom this kind of adaptation of what they have learned, or extemporization to fit their audience, may come hard. And for these student teachers, training must emphasize just this or it is totally wasted.

Both in primary and in secondary training, then, there is much room for improvement. How can this be brought about? In general terms, the solution must be to involve schools more and more in the training of teachers, leaving a different role to colleges of higher education and to polytechnic and university departments of education. Indeed, the centre of training must shift from institutions of higher education to the schools themselves. Wherever such involvement is greatest, the Inspectors find the greatest practical value in the training. Moreover, if practising teachers take responsibility for the training of their junior colleagues, this will necessarily entail a proper professionalism among teachers themselves, which is what is most to be desired. Teachers should no longer have to behave as if someone else, someone higher up the ladder, was the final arbiter of what is needed to make a 'good teacher'.

In the first place, schools, and teachers within them, should be responsible for the selection of candidates for teaching, whether school-leavers aiming to enter the profession through the B.Ed., or, perhaps more importantly, university or polytechnic-leavers aiming to qualify through the PGCE. In this way a more realistic set of criteria could be used, and a good deal of wastage avoided.

Secondly, the training of teachers should be separated from the pursuit of higher education in general. If the B.Ed. is to continue and be more effective there must be an intensive first-year course in a variety of academic subjects, treated not with special reference to teaching but in a general way which could be broadly described as 'philosophical', the emphasis being on the interrelation of one subject to another, and the presuppositions lying behind the study of all of them. After this, specific training should begin, carried out both in college and in the class-room itself. Practising teachers could be responsible for the greatest part of the training, whether in class or in the schools, and students, based in schools, should keep school not university terms. Gradually throughout the course the student teacher should take more and more responsibility for the actual conduct of classes, all the time subject to comment, analysis, and assessment by practising teachers. None but primary school teachers should be trained by the B.Ed., and not all of those. An increasing number of primary and all secondary teachers should read a degree course at university or polytechnic, and then proceed to the PGCE. In the case of the PGCE it is of even more crucial importance that the main part of the single training year should be spent not on theory but on practice, and that the student should be firmly based in a school throughout his course.

In order to make school-based work the central feature of professional training there should be, in every area, certain designated 'teaching schools', both primary and secondary, on an analogy with the teaching hospitals that are an accepted part of medical training. These schools would be so structured that they could accommodate a number of student teachers every year in a variety of different subjects. The students would be under the tutelage of certain designated teacher-tutors who would devote half their time to teaching students, half to teaching children in the school. Some of their tutorial work would consist in delivering lectures or holding seminars in their local colleges or departments of educational studies; some would be a matter of attending student teachers' lessons, and giving individual tutorials arising out of these lessons.

Colleges of higher education (if they continue to exist) and departments of education in universities and polytechnics should concentrate on educational research and on practical training to an equal extent; but their staff should be almost totally interchangeable with the staff of schools, especially the staff of the new teaching schools. Already there are seen to be enormous benefits to schools wherever lecturers from departments in local universities undertake part-time teaching in schools. The advantages would be equally great the other way round.

At present it is extremely difficult to move between the school and the university or polytechnic sector of education. There is no system of transferable pensions; and, at least in the case of the universities, there is no common employer. But it would not be difficult to devise a system that would make such crossover possible and normal. A teacher-tutor would be a specific and senior person who would be employed equally by the Local Education Authority (or board of governors or whoever was the employer of schoolteachers) and the institution of higher education to which the school was attached. The establishment of such posts would not only vastly improve the standard of teacher training; it would also offer a new road of advancement for a good teacher, who would be able to enhance his own career within the profession while maintaining his connections with the class-room. A scheme very like this is actually in operation (or, more accurately, coming into operation, stage by stage) in some schools in Oxfordshire.[9] Schools are invited to apply to the Department of Educational Studies if they wish to take part. If they are chosen to do so, they will receive a group of 8 to 12 students studying for the PGCE, in pairs, two to a subject. These 'interns' will spend a considerable part of their time in their year of training in the host school. They will have some weeks of 'block' training in the school but, for the most part, they will be working at school and in the Department concurrently. In school they will be looked after by a mentor, one to each pair of students, who will be responsible for their day-to-day class-room activity, ensuring that they both teach and observe in the most profitable way in their particular subject. They will also have a professional tutor, a designated member of the school staff who accepts a co-ordinating responsibility for the whole group of interns on the school, and all their non-subject-specific work. In the Department the mentor and professional tutor will be matched by a curriculum tutor and a general tutor who will work in close collaboration with the schools where the interns are placed. Since there are in the Department a number of schoolteachers on secondment each year, who form a 'Development Group' and who work on various aspects of the internship scheme, it seems that students are in contact more with schoolteachers than with university lecturers; and this, I believe, is how it should be. Another similar scheme has long been operated at the King's College London Centre for Educational Studies.

Schemes such as these appear to be working very well. But if they are to develop with any security they must become mandatory in all parts of the country, and funding must be assured jointly by the University Grants Committee (or its successor funding body) and the LEA, or other teacher-employing agencies. If the scheme developed as it should, the university departments would become, as far as the PGCE students go, little more than enabling and co-ordinating bodies. But alongside this they would have an essential and increasing function in educational research, curricular innovation, and the construction and monitoring of new examinations. The relation between schools and universities will change; but it will not be, for that reason, less close.

Such a change as this would mean that teachers became ultimately responsible for the selection and training of their own professionals. Not only would this improve the status and morale of teachers, but it would ensure that training was up to date and realistic. Both these advantages, though they would be manifest throughout the school system, would perhaps bring the most immediate benefits to the primary schools. For at present those who train teachers in colleges are, as we have seen, very often far out of touch with the actual teaching of young children; and those who teach in primary schools tend to be the most despised by society at large, simply on the grounds that their pupils are young, and the content of the curriculum they teach not 'advanced' or 'learned' in academic terms. At present the assumption is that the older the pupil, the higher the status of his teacher. It is as if we were to accord greater respect to geriatric physicians than to paediatricians. We must learn that the teaching of young children is a technically difficult task, and one that should be respected, where it is well done, as much as the teaching of secondary school children or adults.

Both for primary and for secondary school student teachers, the year of the PGCE is all too short. However, it is not realistic to suggest that it should be extended beyond a year. That being so, it is essential that the content of the course should be practical, wide-ranging, and up to date. There will be no time during the year for extended courses of lectures on the history or philosophy of education. There is too much that needs to be learned, at the most basic level, about child-development, the setting and marking of examinations, and about class-room management. I do not mean to argue that the history and philosophy of education do not have a right to exist as academic subjects. But academic is what they are; and they should be studied in universities and polytechnics by those who may, quite properly, want a higher degree in education (perhaps leading to a post either in university teaching or, let us say, in the educational psychology service). For those who aim to teach in school, there will be enough, and more than enough, to fill the PGCE course without engaging in subjects that are entirely theoretical or historical.

After this year has been satisfactorily completed, partly in college, partly in the class-room, with an examination and an assessment based on work within a school, the student teacher should be awarded a certificate, but should not yet be licensed to teach. A further year, or better still two years, as a probationer teacher should be completed satisfactorily before a teacher is actually accredited to practise. This is to suggest that the probationary year should, if possible, be extended to two years, but, more important, that it should be taken far more seriously than it often is today. If candidates for the profession had been selected carefully, and by people who were themselves engaged in school-teaching, there might not be many failures; but there would be some. Such people, who did not win their accreditation, would, on this scheme, have both their original degree (BA or B.Sc.) and a PGCE. The combination of these qualifications could be useful in all kinds of work: publishing, industry, broadcasting, journalism, and many other fields. One would not be rejecting a student teacher who would then be unemployable. But such a serious probationary period would ensure a far higher standard among young teachers than we have now. The probationary years would be closely monitored and assessed by a teacher tutor, or by the college-based tutor whom the probationer had worked under when he was doing his PGCE. Immediately after he had successfully completed his probationary period, the young teacher would get a substantial increase in salary, and would be a fully fledged teacher. But even after this he would have his work assessed annually by senior teachers in his school, and by advisers in the Local Authority; and these assessors would also be people who would be interested in the development of his career. Such a proposal would not necessarily be in conflict with Mr Baker's scheme (announced in May 1988) that there should be licensed teachers drawn from a variety of spheres such as industry, who, in virtue of their special knowledge, might be licensed to teach for a fixed number of years, in shortage subjects. After 1992 it might be that teachers will come over from Europe to teach languages, and be similarly licensed to teach. As long as a shortage of graduates willing to go into teaching persists, such a scheme seems inevitable, and in any case not wholly to be deplored, so long as the standards of performance of such teachers is monitored and professionalism demanded.

There should, as part of the career structure of teachers, be continuous training opportunities. I do not believe that in-service training need be expensive. Teachers who were ambitious would be prepared to pay for their own in-service training, provided that such training carried a career benefit, a certificate, or other qualification which would have financial consequences and would, in the long run, enhance the opportunities for those who had taken the course. But the training would have to be part-time, in evening lectures, or else arranged for the holidays; for it is certain that arranging substitute teaching for colleagues who go on courses is both expensive and often very unsatisfactory for members of a school.

I have so far spoken of better training as the means to the proper professionalization of teachers. And this is certainly a most important aspect of the matter, and the one that can perhaps be most easily achieved. But there are two other related factors of almost equal importance.

First, it is essential that teachers should unite in a common professional enterprise, and impose on themselves common professional standards, by forming a General Teaching Council. This idea has been discussed at great length and over a great many years. There are numbers of teachers who are deeply committed to it and who would like nothing better than to see it become a reality. It is difficult to see what objections there are to the establishing of such a council. The strongest teachers' unions perhaps distrust the concept as a diminution of their power; and there are those among primary school teachers who may distrust it (though many support it strongly) for fear that they would be somehow out-voted on any such council, or at least that their concerns would be generally neglected by it. But such fears would not be difficult to allay, and, in any case, could not be proved groundless except by the setting up of the council. At all events, it is absolutely essential that there be such a council if the teaching profession is to be respected and trusted, if it is to have as much authority as lawyers and doctors, who have such central bodies—the source, for those professions, both of agreed standards of practice and of discipline.

If a General Teaching Council were to be set up, its first task would be to establish criteria for good practice. It would have powers to monitor the performance of teachers at various stages of their careers, to receive complaints of unprofessional conduct or incompetence, and it would ultimately have the power to 'strike off' those who fell below the standards laid down. The council would be composed of teachers both from the maintained and the independent sectors, and from both primary and secondary schools. It might have a small lay membership, and some members from higher and further education. Its chairmanship should be a rotating office, held by primary and secondary teachers in turn.

Working in conjunction with the DES, the council would be responsible for accrediting teachers after they had completed their probationary period following the PGCE or B.Ed. awarded by their university. It would establish criteria for good teaching conduct in such matters as political neutrality, the impartial treatment of different races, the awareness of pupils' special needs, the keeping of records, the marking of pupils' work, and the continuous assessment of pupils for examination purposes. It would thus have a strong influence on the training of teachers, and would, indeed, be empowered to lay down a common curriculum for this training. The time is absolutely right for the foundation of a Teaching Council.

The second reform that is necessary, if the teaching profession is to be fit to provide the education system we need, is that there should be a restructuring of teachers' salaries. Although the removal of 'negotiating rights' over pay and conditions has been a matter of extreme contention between teachers and government, and although at the time of writing it is unclear who will be the employer of teachers, whether government or Local Authorities or private educational trusts, in fact these matters are of far less importance in the long run than that somehow the salary structure both within primary and secondary schools should be rationalized and improved for all types of school. All talk of professionalism is idle unless those entering the teaching service can see a proper development of their career before them, with proper rewards. What is needed is not a general pay rise to be distributed equally among all, but a system of pay differentials depending not on some whim of headmaster or Local Authority but on the teachers' own common criteria. Whether a teacher works in a primary or a secondary school the differentials should be progressive, and the difference between the bottom and the top salaries should be much greater than it is now. It must be made worthwhile for a teacher to be ambitious, whether he aims to become a head, or a teacher tutor, or head of a large department. Teachers are not very badly off when they enter the profession at present, compared with, say, barristers or doctors or journalists. But the top salary that they can reach is ridiculously low compared with that of other professions. A senior teacher ought to be able to be compared with a civil servant of the same age, or a general practitioner, or the managing director of a medium-sized firm.

In West Germany the headteacher of a *Gymnasium* (a

grammar school with over 360 pupils) is paid the same as a civil servant who would be the equivalent to our assistant secretary. That is about £7,000 a year more than a similar headmaster would earn in this country. It seems to me that it is of the utmost importance that we take a decision to pay senior teachers on this kind of scale, whether they teach in primary or in secondary schools. Only so can people entering teaching do so in the confidence that, if they work hard, they can earn a salary that is worthy of respect. For there is no doubt that what a person earns is an important factor in establishing his status in society. This is a fact, and it cannot be changed. It is not satisfactory if the only people willing to embark on teaching as a career are either those who feel themselves incapable of making a living in the competitive world of commerce/industry or the City, or those who go in for it out of charity, a sense of duty, or a general lack of sympathy with the so-called rat race. Teaching should not be a form of 'do-gooding' (though it does do immense good). It should be a profession that is in every way rewarding to enter, and for which no one needs to apologize. There is a real sense in which we get the teachers we are prepared to pay for. Only if these reforms can be brought about will the standard of education at school itself improve; only so will there come into existence the kind of partnership between parents and teachers, both involved in a common enterprise, that will ensure the best education for children.

But there is another reason why the status and the self-confidence of teachers must be improved. Perhaps even more important than the relation between school and parents is the relation between school and tertiary education, FE colleges, polytechnics, and universities. If education in this country is to improve then we must learn to think of it as *one* system. There must be a genuine partnership between teachers at all of the stages of education. This cannot come about as long as some members of the teaching profession regard themselves, resentfully, as notably inferior or worse off than others. Universities and schools must think of themselves as having a common cause. It is time to turn now to the place of tertiary education in the system as a whole.

Higher education

The old and absolute distinctions between the different stages of education have to a certain extent broken down. The close connection between primary and secondary school is obvious enough; and the connection will become even closer as teachers from the two stages of school begin to regard themselves more and more as members of a single professional body, more of them university or polytechnic educated, and all bound by a single set of professional standards. Meanwhile, at the other end, the distinction between secondary and tertiary education has already become somewhat obscure, with fewer pupils abandoning education at 16, more training courses starting in the school class-room, and vocationalism extending its grip at an ever earlier age. In the new 1980s-style tertiary colleges a variety of courses go on side by side, from traditional A level, pre-university courses, to B.Tech., retraining, and, in theory at least, adult education.

I am concerned in this chapter with higher education, that which is on offer at universities and polytechnics. But I shall argue that it is impossible to think about this sector, or make predictions about its future, without considering it too as a part of the whole educational provision of the country. There is a sense in which, just as for any individual, education is a continuous process, so the institutions that provide it form a seamless web. Yet, perhaps paradoxically, I shall also argue that, within the total educational system, universities and polytechnics must continue to regard themselves as quite different from schools and tertiary colleges, and that degree-awarding institutions, though part of the whole, must to some extent be a law to themselves.

Before going on to either part of this argument, I must acknowledge a quite general difficulty. It is hard for anyone who works in a university to seem to speak with a dispassionate voice about higher education. This is not a phenomenon peculiar to universities; if the proprietor of a village shop discussed the role of such shops in rural life; if a clergyman of the Church of England argued against the disestablishment of the Church, people would regard what was said with the same kind of scepticism: 'He would say that, wouldn't he?' This is an unanswerable question and one intended simply to render any argument that may be used suspect from the outset on account of its source. No one, it is suggested, can be taken seriously as an analyst of a particular tradition or institution unless he is an outsider. If he is an insider he is bound to wish so strongly to preserve the status quo that his judgement is warped, his eyes blinkered. There will be nothing but special pleading. Since I cannot take away from myself the years I have spent as a member of a university, I must simply note the inevitable response, and proceed with the argument.

To what extent, then, should higher education be treated as part of the educational provision, with interests identical to those of schools and tertiary colleges? Those school-leavers entering higher education (defined, as I have said, as that which is provided by universities and polytechnics) still form a minority of the whole age-group. The figures published by the DES in 1987 show that degrees or higher diplomas were awarded in the whole of the UK to 27 per cent of the relevant age-group in 1986 (this figure includes degrees and diplomas awarded to graduates from colleges of higher education as well as universities and polytechnics; and their numbers are not negligible).[1] This contrasts with the Japanese figure of 35 per cent and the American of 32 per cent, but is higher than that of any other European country. In the 1987 White Paper *Higher Education: Meeting the Challenge* it was proposed that there should be a 5 per cent increase in student numbers up to the year 1990, followed by a return to current levels in the mid-1990s, when the relevant age-group would be smallest, followed again by a further increase. But it was acknowledged that a number of factors might determine the actual numbers in higher education during this period, including the success or otherwise of the schools in increasing pass rates in examinations.

One way and another, then, at most a third of those leaving school are expected to be going on to higher education even by the end of the century. But this third cannot any longer be thought of as a specially privileged élite. And their education is, and will continue to be, an expense that the public must at least partially meet. It is therefore perfectly proper that society in general should expect to understand and broadly approve of the education it is paying for. Just as in the 1940s secondary education became a right to which all children were entitled up to the age of 15 and which had to be provided out of the public purse, so in the 1960s, in accordance with the recommendations of the Robbins Committee,[2] higher education was taken on as a right for all those who were qualified (with two A levels) and who wanted it. It is unthinkable that any government should altogether go back on such a commitment. Student grants are mandatory: students are not luxuriously provided for; indeed government itself has admitted that their grants, severely cut in real terms since the beginning of the 1980s, are no longer adequate.

It is now proposed that a system of loans be introduced, at least as a supplement to student grants. The loan system in the United States is often mentioned as a good parallel and one which works. But I am not sure how encouraging the parallel is. In the first place, though a high proportion of school leavers enter higher education in the US a very great number drop out after a year, and it is not clear how many do so on financial grounds. Secondly, the difficulty of persuading graduates into badly paid jobs such as teaching is even greater than it is here. Certainly in this country a young teacher (or social worker, say) would have enormous difficulty in paying back his loan, especially as the cost of housing gets higher and higher. There would be vast numbers of defaulters except among those whose parents could help them pay. A system of loans might in the end prove highly discriminatory.

So there is no way out of it: higher education must be paid for publicly. In addition, the provision of teaching, especially in the sciences, has become increasingly expensive. Government must fund both individuals and institutions. Thus universities and polytechnics must be publicly accountable for what they provide just as schools are. They must not only publish their accounts, but must be prepared to demonstrate to the world that they offer 'value for money'.

In this respect the position of higher education is no different from that of education at school. But the task of the institutions of higher education is harder. For, though parents may complain about schools, and may despise those who teach in them, there is a more widespread and deeper hostility among the public to higher education. So slowly do attitudes change that many people regard universities as places which the rich and spoiled can join for the asking, and where gilded youth can idle away its time in punts, with glasses full of champagne, at the public expense. The television adaptation of *Brideshead Revisited*, brilliantly evocative of an Oxford none of us remembers except vicariously, was taken by many of its viewers as a literal and accurate depiction of Oxford as it is today (and it has to be admitted that this impression was confirmed by the numbers of undergraduates who immediately began to dress up as Sebastian Flyte: long overcoats, diamond-patterned socks, pale Fair Isle pullovers, became a uniform overnight). On the other hand students of all kinds, both in universities and polytechnics, acquired a different sort of reputation for idleness in the late 1960s and 1970s. They were seen as disruptive, work-shy, and, above all, dangerously politicized; and though times have totally changed since then, this quite different source of fear and dislike also remains. Emotions ossify and attitudes are hard to change. The very word 'student' is an irritant.

Not only students but teachers in universities are subject to these two contradictory sources of dislike. On the one hand they are considered dangerously far to the left and slavish Marxists. On the other hand they are held to be rich, self-indulgent, and totally ignorant of work and the world. Small wonder that when we complain about government treatment of the universities we get no reaction except exasperation. For example, at the beginning of 1986 John Clare, the BBC Education Correspondent, uttered a long tirade against the universities. He ended by quoting with approval the remark made by a Government spokesman that the universities have few friends. 'Do they ever', he said, 'ask themselves why?'[3]

Education as a whole is not much valued by either public or government; higher education least of all. It is all the more important that the universities and polytechnics should genuinely work *with* the secondary schools, and be seen to do so, for the benefit of their pupils. No one thinks of schoolchildren as idle drones, nor yet as politically dangerous agitators (though their teachers are sometimes so described). Pupils do not suddenly change overnight when they go to university, and the continuity must be made clear.

The institutions of higher education must therefore change their attitude towards the transition from school. Despite the general commitment to provide places in higher education for all who are qualified and who wish to apply, there is no doubt that entry to some universities and polytechnics, and in some subjects, is highly competitive and is likely to remain so. This fact has tended to place secondary and higher education on opposite sides of a fence, the grass on the university side being gazed at with envy by those on the school side. From the standpoint of schoolteachers, too, those who teach in universities are envied and often distrusted. The gulf between secondary and higher education is made virtually impossible for teachers to cross by the different salary system, deriving from different sources, and especially by the absence of transferable pensions from one side of the divide to the other.

There has been in the past a long history of snobbishness, graft, old boys' network, and doubtless other suspect influences at work, especially in the admission of undergraduates to Oxford and Cambridge colleges when those were predominantly for men and predominantly for candidates from independent schools. Even the women's colleges, though they had nothing like the same sort of network, used to admit an unduly large number of candidates from independent and direct-grant schools, mainly because so high a proportion of their applicants came from such schools. The college entrance examinations were generally, though by no means universally, thought to entail an extra term in the sixth form, and this only the independent schools could be certain to provide. Things have changed, and now, though Oxford has retained an optional entrance examination, it is no longer taken in a seventh sixth-form term;

and Cambridge has abandoned the entrance examination altogether and come into line with other universities and polytechnics in demanding A levels only. As usual the full extent of the changes has not been widely understood, and there is still a sense that the universities, particularly Oxford and Cambridge, are demanding something that the schools can only with difficulty provide. Moreover, it is commonly held that whatever the university entrance requirements may be, candidates from independent schools will have a better chance of defeating the system, and so will be awarded places that they do not properly deserve. This increases the sense that battle is being waged each year between schools and universities.

Because there seems to be less of a battle between schools and polytechnics, the securing of a place in a polytechnic is less highly prized in schools, and this is a pity, since many polytechnic courses are better than equivalent courses at university and just as difficult to get onto. In the 1950s we used to hear about 'parity of esteem' between grammar schools and secondary modern schools: it is more important now that there should be 'parity of esteem' among institutions of higher education. This is another reason for thinking of higher education as a whole, and as part of the whole educational provision.

On their side, the universities especially have made things worse by their inability to envisage change. In 1970, when new universities were still springing up, Lord James of Rusholme, then Vice-Chancellor of York, predicted that the further expansion of higher education would be a dominant feature of the next decade, and he voiced doubts about what he foresaw. He was anxious lest, out of a proper desire for equality, the spread of higher education would be allowed to damage its quality. At much the same time Kingsley Amis, then a university teacher, stated firmly, and with a conviction that was widely shared, that 'More means Worse'. Though we no longer fear indiscriminate expansion, indeed are more afraid of enforced contraction, the spirit of Kingsley Amis is still alive. In the universities, like the British in India as they changed nightly into their dinner jackets, we tend to talk about 'keeping up the standards'. The most obvious and visible way to do this, though it is a very crude way, is to demand from candidates for admission higher and higher grades at A level. Sometimes universities and polytechnics have actually been themselves graded in some scale of excellence or worthiness of support according to the A level grades of their undergraduates. But this policy is becoming ever more un-satisfactory as time goes on. In the first place, increasingly, the candidates who are sure to get the high grades demanded tend to be those from independent schools where the staff/pupil ratio is favourable to small A level classes and to intensive coaching. The proportion of university students coming from independent schools is slowly creeping up again, reinforcing the popular perception of universities as élitist and only for the rich. At the same time the relevance of A levels to university and polytechnic education is diminishing. Those with the best A level grades do not necessarily get the best degrees, especially in subjects such as law, history, philosophy, or economics. Nor are three As at A level any guarantee that a student will be able to manage a mathematics or engineering course in some of our major univer-sities. Finally, with the introduction of the GCSE, it is widely ex-pected that A levels themselves may change in unpredictable ways, despite the apparent determination of government to preserve them unchanged.

I have discussed the new examination system and some of its implications in Chapter 3. Without returning to the subject in detail, I must refer again to the apparently paradoxical insistence of the Secretary of State that, though all else has changed, A levels must not change. This paradox is directly relevant to the question of access to higher education. In his letter to the Higginson Committee Kenneth Baker mentioned the need to consider wider implications, notably the approaches to teaching, learning, and assessment to which pupils will have become used in GCSE courses. He spoke hopefully of 'the need for breadth and balance of knowledge and understanding within each syllabus, without sacrificing depth of study' and finally he called attention to 'the relevance of alternative routes to Higher Education'. All this might seem to indicate a fairly flexible ap-proach to the question of selection for higher education. And it may turn out that the Committee itself will make recommendations for change. It is extremely doubtful, however, whether the universities as a whole will show themselves willing to adapt. Certainly the University of Cambridge, replying to a request for comments from the Higginson Committee, welcomed the terms of reference of the Committee, which they took to indicate that 'standards' would be maintained, if not elevated, and went on to expound the need for ensuring that candidates for places in the University had as much knowledge as before, especially in the sciences. In my opinion (an opinion not shared by many of my colleagues), to respond in this way was to miss an opportunity of opening up new ways to select candidates for places. Still more important, the response was tantamount to a refusal to consider whether the courses for which the candidates were applying might not themselves be in need of revision. The general attitude, exemplified not only in this reply to Higginson but in many informal discussions within the University and the Colleges, has been that Cambridge (and I cite Cambridge only because I am familiar with it) *cannot* change, and sees no reason to do so. Therefore schools, and school-based examinations, must somehow or other conform to the standards demanded by the University. This attitude has been the bane of school examinations and assessment for years. It is supported only by the semi-magical incantation of the word 'standards'.

There are two ways in which the universities could and should have responded. First, without in any way undertaking to change their degree courses, they could allow that candidates might present themselves for entry who were less well equipped with factual knowledge than in the past. They could therefore accept candidates on condition that they attended a pre-entry course, lasting perhaps a month, and held at the University itself, in which pupils would be taught intensively in order to familiarize them both with certain areas they might not have covered at all at school, and with the general method of teaching and learning that they would encounter during their years as undergraduates. These courses would be a necessary part of the whole University course, and would take place, let us say, in August or September, before the University term started; they should be paid for out of the student grant which should be increased to cover them. Satisfactory completion of the course would be the final condition of entry for any student. It is astonishing how much can be taught in a month to people who are motivated to learn, and who are being taught with a specific goal in mind. In this case the goal would differ from one subject to another; but all the goals would be attainable by a keen student and an energetic teacher. There would be an enormous advantage, in that when the first regular term began students could be presumed all to have the necessary background information (or know where to look it up) and the necessary skills. Thus, for example, when all those about to embark on a degree course in economics assembled at the beginning of term none would be wholly ignorant of statistical method, even though for some their knowledge might be slight and recently acquired.

I would like to see it as a regular part of the duties of university lecturers or tutors to provide such teaching, either undertaking it themselves or engaging graduate students to do it for them, if, let us say, they were themselves busy finishing a book or engaged in research abroad. But, in general, the responsibility should be theirs. And it would be good for them to have to teach, for this month, at an elementary level, becoming acquainted for themselves with the weaknesses, but also the strengths, of pupils barely out of school.

The second response, not incompatible with the first, but more radical and inevitably, if undertaken, more gradual, would be to consider some changes in the courses on offer to undergraduates at university. I believe that there is need for such changes and that sooner or later they will have to come. Roughly speaking, universities and polytechnics, like schools themselves, should begin consciously to give priority to method rather than content, to a specific manner of acquiring and dealing with information rather than the information itself; and this method should be taught by practice, not by theory. Such changes will be more radical, more difficult to bring about, and more strongly resisted in some courses than in others. For at many universities method is already the most important aspect of the curriculum in certain areas. An Oxford history graduate, for example, may be quite ignorant of large stretches of history. It may indeed be irritating to ask him some question about, say, seventeenth-century France and find that he knows nothing at all about it, expert though he may be about fourteenth-century England. But what he *will* have is both an awareness of how to find out the nature of historical problems and an ability to distinguish good evidence from bad in seeking solutions. In addition he will have acquired the ability to write and argue for his own interpretations. His skills will be genuinely transferable.

What I suggest is that such outcomes should be more clearly recognized and more boldly stated as the purpose of any course, and should be reflected in the assessment of undergraduates at the end of the course. It follows, then, that access to higher education should be granted to those candidates who can show by their past record that they are capable of acquiring such skills and putting them to use of whatever kind. This means that when they apply for entry, candidates need not necessarily have a great deal of knowledge of the specific subject they want to pursue. They need only have the ability to apply themselves to the underlying principles of that subject, and to express themselves clearly and intelligently. This last is something that schools should concern themselves with, as their primary responsibility.

There are two further points to be made, both concerned with access to higher education and the question who should be selected for it. First, a policy decision needs to be made about overseas students. This is not, as it might seem, a merely peripheral point, but is central to higher educational policy. Since 1979, when the general subsidy of all overseas students was withdrawn and they began to pay full fees for higher education, there has been no clear decision about which students should be encouraged to come, and for which courses. At one time the University Grants Committee kept an eye on the numbers admitted by any one university, to ensure that departments were not overloaded, but they have now given this up, and in practice universities and polytechnics tend to tout for custom, since the fees overseas students pay have become essential 'free' money, enabling the institutions to keep their financial heads above water. Some overseas students still receive government subsidy in the form of bursaries, but the recipients are selected on grounds of political expediency, 'aid' requirements, or commercial reciprocity, not in accordance with academic criteria. No government is likely to return to the pre-1979 levels of subsidy, sincerely though its withdrawal was regretted at the time. As the *Times Higher Education Supplement* put it:

However murky the origin and confused the operation of the Government's present policy on overseas students, its outline is unlikely to be changed. In general overseas students will be charged the full cost of their higher or further education, but selected students will have their tuition subsidized. This policy is the only show in town, and there are no future bookings.[4]

Financial considerations apart, there is a vague feeling that it is a good idea to have overseas students. But it is less than clear with whom the advantage is supposed to lie, with them or with us. If we were to formulate a policy laying down clearly what was on offer at different institutions, what it would cost, and what mutual benefits (including perhaps exchange visits) might arise, then we could ourselves become more certain what higher education was supposed to be for, and we might get away from the slightly shifty, hole-and-corner attitude we now adopt towards offering something so manifestly beneficial to ourselves. If the concept of flexibility, or transferable skills, were central to our higher education policy as a whole, this might be something quite specifically attractive to overseas students. Less clear thoughts about the Home Country, or the British Heritage could be thrown in as a bonus, but need not form the sole justification for accepting university and polytechnic students from abroad. It would be good for us, and for potential students from abroad, if we could clarify what is on offer.

The second point is far more obviously important. It is concerned with access to universities and polytechnics for mature students and others who do not come straight from school. The 1987 White Paper *Higher Education: Meeting the Challenge* emphasized the need for institutions of higher education to accept students who will come in by routes other than that of A levels, and especially to make provision for those with the new vocational, rather than academic, qualifications. It also suggests a rationalization of 'access courses' for those who hold no qualifications at all.[5] Among those for whom access courses should be especially designed are mature students. The suggestion is that the numbers of such students in regular academic courses can be considerably increased without any lowering of academic standards. On present evidence, this is true. Mature students at least tend to be well motivated, sensible, and articulate, and they often add a great deal to any 'year' of which they are part, though they sometimes have considerable and understandable difficulty in doing themselves full justice in their final examinations. They are often too slow and self-critical to fling themselves into the marathon of three-hour papers with their juniors.

But besides these regular, if elderly, undergraduates, the White Paper also calls attention to the need for more continuing and adult education, dividing this broadly into the vocational (training or retraining in mid-career) and the non-vocational (for personal satisfaction or for 'leisure'). The question must be raised to what extent institutions of higher education can contribute to this kind of education and training. Such education is essentially designed for people with a particular, perhaps a limited, need. These students cannot be treated just like ordinary undergraduates, differentiated only by their age: they are not 'deemed' to be 18-year-olds, like the group mentioned above. For them a different kind of provision is required. And if we are to consider higher education in the context of education as a whole, from primary school onwards, it is necessary to see where, if at all, institutions that supply higher education can fit in to the increasing demands for education as something that must be supplied, on and off, throughout the whole life of an individual.

Most universities have departments of adult education (or extra-mural departments, as they are still sometimes called), and there is a variety of ways in which these are funded; through the DES, the UGC, or by fees paid by individuals or Local Education Authorities. But most of the work in these departments, which is often of a high standard, is in arts subjects, and much would fall into the non-vocational, 'leisure' class specified by the White Paper. Few departments have any access to laboratories. Thus a full contribution to continuing education, especially in the vocational category, must involve the institution, university or polytechnic, as a whole, not just the adult education departments, important though these departments will continue to be.

In a volume of essays published in 1985, *Widening the Field: Continuing Education in Higher Education*, Pat Fleetwood-Walker and Peter Taylor (in an essay entitled 'Jam Today') discuss the reports produced in the previous year by both the UGC and the National Advisory Body on the future of continuing education. Both reports are found to be generally optimistic about the role that institutions of higher education can play in supplying the identified need, even in the field of vocational training and retraining. The authors of the article conclude that the greatest obstacle to progress is the attitude of the academics within the institutions, and their unwillingness to adapt.[6] In the same volume Tyrrell Burgess outlines a scheme by which an individual coming into an institution of higher education, perhaps part-time or for a short continuous spell, could be given credits or certification for work done within an ordinary department, in accordance with a purpose-made programme suiting his needs.[7] The argument is that higher education must concern itself not only with degree courses but with detachable bits of courses, modules, which can be taken by students for whom they will be useful at any stage of their career, and coming from any background. Such a proposal is by no means easy to implement. There are inevitable problems about access to laboratories, space in libraries, provision of supervisors, to say nothing of the difficulties involved in creating genuinely free-standing modular courses to be selected, like sweets off the sweet-trolley, regardless of their relation to a whole curriculum.

If establishments of higher education are to contribute something genuinely useful in this field, especially when vocational education is in question, it seems to me plain that the initiative must come not from individuals, nor from the establishments themselves, but from industry or other employing bodies. For there is by now a good deal of depressing evidence that people who acquire qualifications in mid-career simply because they decide to do so (and this applies especially to married women) find it very difficult thereafter to find work. Though they may have enjoyed their belated education and have benefited from it personally, they are unlikely to fit into any employment slot as a result of it. Again, institutions themselves are unlikely to be successful in training under their own initiative, since their expertise is properly academic and theory-based, and cannot be expected to be totally up to date with regard to the needs of particular industries. Writing in the *Oxford Magazine* in the summer of 1986, Stephen Bungay, an Oxford-educated management consultant, said this:

Training in specific skills is the responsibility of the employer, not universities [or polytechnics, he might have added]. Universities cannot conceivably act as training institutions. Neither would the best employers have it so, for they realize that the quality of their training schemes is a potential source of competitive advantage, and are concerned to train in their own way of doing things, to instil their ethics and their values.

But to accept this is not to deny the possibility of fruitful partnership between employers and establishments of higher education. An effective training scheme within a company requires highly educated trainers, who may have to be retrained themselves in mid-career to fulfil such a function. There may also arise specific training demands when a new process is introduced and technicians need to be made familiar not simply with the process itself but with the theory that lies behind it. In such cases special arrangements can be made with universities and polytechnics to set up short courses, and both to teach and to assess those who go on them. There is no doubt that in such ways as this, as well as in a willingness to accept mature students for full degree courses, seconded from particular companies, universities and polytechnics have an increasing part to play, and must advertise their realization of this fact.

So far in this chapter I have been concerned with the respects in which higher education must be seen as part of the total educational provision of the country, from the nursery even as far as the old people's home, and how it may have to adapt to fulfil the perfectly legitimate demands made on it by government and society at large. I must now say something about the nature of higher education and its overall purposes in comparison with other sorts of education; and this in turn will lead to the question of its degree of independence. How free should our universities and polytechnics be? What are the limits, if any, of their accountability?

The discussion of access to higher education in the preceding pages will have made it plain that any improvement in higher education provision depends crucially on an improvement in school education. If we think of the superiority of Japan over ourselves, both in access to higher education and in the outcome of it, we have to remember first of all the superiority of their school system, and the amount of government money spent on it. In a comparison between Japanese and American education the anthropologist Thomas Rohlen wrote:

> The Japanese go to school one third more time than do Americans every year . . . They don't lose during long summer vacations half of what they have learned the previous year. Elementary education takes them further in the basics, as well as in art and music, compared with our schools . . . The great accomplishment of Japanese primary and secondary education does not lie in its creation of a brilliant élite (Western nations do better with their top students) but in its generation of such a high average level of capability. The profoundly impressive fact is that it is shaping a whole population, workers as well as managers, to a standard inconceivable in the United States where we are still trying to implement High School graduation competence tests that measure only minimal reading and computing skills.[8]

Five years on we could say the same about this country.

As I have argued, it is useless to attempt to improve the standard in our schools without a highly educated and respected professional force of teachers, and one of the main purposes of higher education must be to provide teachers who will go out into the schools. This must be a key part of our common policy. For the connection works both ways; we cannot hope for more co-operation between schools and establishments of higher education, nor for wider access to the latter, unless the schools can be relied upon to teach pupils to work and to think for themselves, in readiness for the next stage.

However, let us suppose that the school system will improve, that standards will rise in the way that government hopes, and that the new examination system will encourage the intellectual development of a wider band of ability than is at present catered for. What will higher education be expected then to provide? What will its new function be, if we see it as the apex of a pyramid of genuinely solid foundation? In the first place, there cannot be just one uniform and identical function for higher education. At present, as those proceeding to higher education from school emerge with a uniform qualification, A levels, it may seem that there must be uniformity at the next stage. If, as I have suggested they should, A levels were to be replaced by graded tests, practical and theoretical, it would be more obvious that those who left school were *variously* competent, and would aspire to a *variety* of different experiences of higher education. Add to that the expected increase in the numbers of those entering higher education by different routes and with avowedly different aims, and it becomes obvious that a uniform kind of higher education would be inadequate.

In order to ensure a wide range of provision we should retain and exploit the somewhat ramshackle distinction we now have between universities and polytechnics, a distinction drawn by the so-called binary line. The essence of this distinction should lie in the nature and content of the education provided in each sector, and in the research undertaken in each.

There has long been a distinction between universities, financed by students' fees (paid for the most part by Local Education Authorities) and by direct grant from government through the UGC, and polytechnics on the other side of the line funded directly by Local Authorities. The growth of the polytechnics in the 1960s changed, but did not create, the distinction between Local Authority responsibility and what was nationally funded. The new polytechnics simply made the Local Authority area larger and stronger. At that time the function of the polytechnics was explicitly defined as different from and complementary to that of the universities. They were to provide technical education and were to devote themselves primarily to producing an expert work-force for industry as it emerged into the era of new technology. Their standard was to be high, and in the vision of the future outlined by, for example, Anthony Crosland, there were to be at least some institutions on this side of the binary line as prestigious as the Massachusetts Institute of Technology or the Polytechnic of Tel Aviv.

From the 1960s onwards, however, it soon became plain that Anthony Crosland's particular vision was not going to be fulfilled. The fact that polytechnics were subject to local control militated against their gaining national, still less international, standing as institutes of technology. But far more important, in the expansionist climate of the 1960s, and caught up in the British disease of snobbishness and the high status of arts compared with that of science and technology, more and more of the polytechnics fell victim to what came to be known as 'academic drift'. The Local Authorities did nothing to stop this drift, indeed may even have encouraged it, as it began to seem that they had universities under a different name in their control. Students at polytechnics read for degrees; but the degree courses had to be approved, and the degree actually awarded either by the CNAA (the Council for National Academic Awards, set up in the 1960s for just this purpose) or, less often, by a neighbouring university if such an arrangement seemed mutually beneficial. The CNAA had no authority to adjudicate on whether or not a proposed degree course, or part-course, were necessary or desirable. All they could do was to try to assess whether, if it came into being, such a course would merit the award of a degree, whether there was adequate teaching, adequate library facilities, and a reasonable supply of candidates to warrant its introduction.

Thus throughout the 1970s polytechnics instituted degree courses in languages, literature, history, philosophy, often narrower and more specialized than would ever have been tolerated in the university sector, and frequently dependent on the whim or empire-building aspirations of a particular lecturer in a particular department. Not all applications for new courses were accepted; but many applications were submitted again and again with specific alterations and emendments in response to CNAA demands. An immense amount of time and money was spent on such submissions. In addition, the CNAA used to mount periodic visitations to the polytechnics and colleges under its charge, and, again, vast sums of money were spent to try to ensure a satisfactory report at the end of the proceedings.

As the polytechnics grew in size and strength (and it has to be remembered that alongside the developments to be accounted for by academic drift there were excellent and exciting developments in the sciences, pure and applied, especially in the interface between science and industry) so the burden of CNAA restrictions became more and more intolerable. In 1984 the Government set up a Committee of Inquiry under the chairmanship of Sir Norman Lindop to examine the whole question of external validation as applied to polytechnics and colleges of higher education. The report of the Committee, *Academic Validation in the Public Sector*, was published the following year, and it recommended a loosening of the bonds of the CNAA almost universally. In the case of some of the large and so-called 'mature' polytechnics it recommended complete freedom to award their own degrees and establish their own courses, subject only to the kinds of checks that universities are subject to, including accountability for cost, and the appointment of external examiners for student examinations. They argued that it was absurd for some of the very best institutions of higher education in the country, such as the Polytechnics of Portsmcuth, Leicester, or Leeds, to name only a few, to be able to take decisions and award degrees only subject to the CNAA, who might find it extremely difficult in some cases to field a validation team as expert as the department they were supposed to be adjudicating.

The Lindop Committee found that although in a few cases polytechnics had been positively damaged by difficulties with their Local Authorities, many, such as the London Polytechnics, already separate bodies and registered charities, had an extremely good relation with the LEA. In any case, complaints from the institutions themselves were far more concerned with the CNAA than with their Local Authorities. Some of the smaller and less well-established institutions, however, valued the authority of the CNAA, both as a prop to their own lack of confidence in their ability to set reasonable standards, and as a stick with which to beat the Local Authority, who might have been inclined to withdraw funds for staff or equipment if the CNAA had not demanded that they be kept up.

Even before the publication of the Lindop report, the CNAA had begun to restrict its activities. It had tentatively embarked on a programme known as 'Partnership in Validation', and had suggested slightly more autonomy for the polytechnics in various subject-areas. But progress was slow. Now, however, its powers and its size have been greatly diminished. Since the setting up in 1981 of the National Advisory Body, to oversee the general distribution of funds to institutions of higher education other than universities, and to make recommendations about common policy, the role of the CNAA has really been confined to the formal one of awarding degrees. It may continue to fulfil that function for a few years yet, but there is no reason why in the foreseeable future it should not wither away. There is no doubt that in the 1960s, at the time of rapid expansion in all sectors of higher education, it did excellent work in ensuring a reasonable uniformity of academic standards throughout the country. Without it the new-born polytechnics might never have been as good as they now are. Now its day is over we should be grateful and let it go.

The 1987 Government White Paper, *Higher Education: Meeting the Challenge*, laid down a radically new support-structure for institutions on both sides of the binary line. Polytechnics and colleges of higher education are to be removed from Local Authority control and made into free-standing bodies in charge of their own funds and their own appointments. Those colleges with fewer than 350 students should remain under the Local Authority, except that those which offer degree courses to more than 55 per cent of their students should be able to choose whether to stay or to free themselves. Voluntary colleges (mostly, originally, Church foundations for the training of teachers) and other grant-aided colleges should also be taken from Local Authority control. All of this sector of institutions, constituting one side of the binary line, will be funded by a new body called the Polytechnic and Colleges Funding Council, which is to enter into contracts with the institutions to provide teaching and research. Contracts for research (and indeed for teaching programmes) may also be entered into with parties other than the PCFC, such as particular, probably local, industries. These recommendations are now incorporated in the Education Reform Bill 1988.

It is laid down that 'the academic work of all the institutions in the new sector will continue to be validated by the CNAA, Universities or the Business and Technical Education Council as appropriate . . .'. But, as I have suggested above, I do not believe that this is right, or that it can last. Validation suggests inferior status, and especially if this were to be undertaken by a university it would be contrary to the spirit of the new binary principle, namely that there should be equality of esteem each side of the line. If the polytechnics are to emerge as true centres of excellence in the applied sciences, both in teaching and research, there is simply no case for forcing upon them a system of external validation that is both time-wasting and expensive. If they are to become in some sense free institutions entrusted with making their own decisions with regard to spending their funds and appointing their staff then they must also be trusted to monitor their own curricula, oversee their own examination practices (with the normal provision of external examiners), and award their own degrees.

However, the colleges of higher education should not be accorded the same status. It is futile to pretend that they can achieve equal esteem in comparison with either universities or polytechnics. Indeed their function is by now highly anomalous. In the old days they were colleges for the training of teachers, and they awarded certificates but not degrees. The new teaching profession has no need of such sub-degree colleges, and so those colleges that have survived have done so by diversifying, but still offering places to a number of people aiming to enter teaching (mostly primary teaching). It is unsatisfactory from the point of view of the teaching profession that their members should be so largely drawn from low-status institutions. I believe that in the end the colleges of higher education will either have to close, or become parts of a neighbouring university or polytechnic (their courses validated by their neighbours), or change their function altogether. They could, for example, most plausibly be used for access courses for those aiming to get into university or polytechnic without formal qualifications. They could also be used as annexes of education departments in universities or polytechnics, where specialist training (for example in the teaching of the deaf or the maladjusted) could be carried out. Although the colleges can neither close nor change their functions immediately, it seems to me clear that this will have to be faced as a long-term policy, if we are to aim at consistency, and a reputable standard throughout the whole of higher education. There are at least thirty colleges to be taken from Local Authority control, and eleven others to which the choice is to be offered whether to free themselves or to stay. Many of these, being already specialist colleges (such as all the colleges of art, of art and design, or of speech and drama), have a role to play that will not change. It is those that have originated out of teacher training colleges and whose degree standards are sometimes embarrassingly low, which will, in my view, have to face dissolution or radical change.

Polytechnics, freed from the control of Local Authorities and freed, as I believe they should be, from the CNAA, will now be ready to seek funds for that which they do best. The system of contracts between institutions of education and funding bodies is new and revolutionary. In the present climate of Government thinking, polytechnics will probably be well advised to seize the chance of reverting to their original role, namely to provide education primarily in applied science and technology and to undertake research in this area, in close liaison with industry, with whom some of their contracts could be made. I do not suggest that nothing but applied science should be taught in polytechnics. This would be impossible. For example, no serious course in any kind of science could be totally divorced from the teaching of mathematics. It is also desirable to have departments of economics and of management and of political theory and philosophy in academic institutions devoted to the applied sciences (MIT is the supreme example of the marriage of such subjects in one institution). But the excellence of the polytechnics in the applied sciences and engineering should be built up and brought to the attention of the public and of industry, as a matter of top priority.

The 1987 White Paper piously said that 'There is no intention that the local and regional links and roles of the institutions concerned [i.e. polytechnics and colleges] should be diminished; on the contrary these should remain a distinctive feature.'[9] Of course in one way these links will have been irrevocably broken. The very land on which the polytechnics stand will have become their own, not the Local Authority's (and already disputes are breaking out about the transfer of such land and other assets).[10] But in other ways the links can remain as strong as before. Industries seeking help with their own programmes of training and retraining will undoubtedly prefer to contract for help with their local polytechnic; and though the best of them will attract students nationally and internationally, sandwich courses and sponsorship may well be locally structured. It is to be hoped that in this way local pride in a local polytechnic will be maintained. This has been one of the great advantages of the old system. Gradually, when central government gets over its fear and detestation of local government the old links may be restored, even reinvented as a bright new idea. But they will be links of a different kind. For the independence of the polytechnics, their freedom to negotiate contracts with industry both for teaching and for research, and an overall freedom to determine the nature of their own degree courses, admissions procedure, and research provision should form a central part of a general educational policy, and it will properly fulfil one part of the function designated by government for higher education. In order that their proper status should be recognized, the freedom of the polytechnics should be as complete as possible.

And so we come to the other side of the binary line, the university sector. Up till now universities have been funded partly by fees from students (paid by Local Authorities), partly by government grants distributed through the University Grants

Committee. The UGC had in the past been a neutral buffer between universities and government, ensuring that universities were not subject to direct political pressure with regard to their expenditure, the establishing of new departments, or the support of old ones. It was the kind of institution of which the British used to be rightly proud (other examples being the Independent Broadcasting Authority, or the Royal Commission on Environmental Pollution), preserving a mixture of independence and control, reporting to and advising government and not wholly subservient to it. However, as government came to exert more and more financial pressure on the universities, the old system of quinquennial grants collapsed, and the UGC became more obviously a branch of the Civil Service, uneasily carrying out government commands, and yet satisfying neither party. In February 1987 a Committee of Inquiry was set up (the Croham Committee) to review the workings of the UGC. The Government accepted a good deal of what this report recommended, and in its own White Paper laid down that funding should henceforth be the responsibility of a Universities Funding Council, parallel to the Funding Council for the Polytechnics and Colleges. Once again, these recommendations became part of the 1988 Education Reform Bill.

There are two important differences between the new arrangements and the old. In the first place, instead of grants to institutions, a system of contracting for services would be set up, so that the UFC will offer contracts or franchises, for which, presumably, the universities will apply, both for teaching specific courses and for research. It is too early to say with any certainty how such a system might work. But it is possible to imagine some sort of rolling contract between a university, let us say the University of Warwick, and the UFC to supply teaching and research in modern history in accordance with certain specific terms relating to the number of students to be taught, the number of lecturers to be employed, and, perhaps, the kind of content and courses to be offered. The University would be subject to periodic scrutiny to ensure that the terms of the contract were being observed (and the UFC would also be constrained by its side of the contract with regard to financial support) and the contract might be terminated at specified break-points if the outcome were not satisfactory. Universities would then be somewhat in the position of commercial radio stations in relation to the Independent Broadcasting Authority: they would have a *limited* freedom to teach and to pursue research, subject to the terms of their contract, but, unlike the radio stations, would be permitted to contract their services to bodies other than the UFC. Indeed, one of the purposes of the system of contracts was explicitly stated to be 'to encourage institutions to be enterprising in attracting contracts from other sources, particularly the private sector, and thereby to lessen their present degree of dependence on public funding'.[11] Thus if some old-established bank, let us say, wished to have its history written, it might contract with the University of Warwick to establish the Coutts Research Centre, for a period of months or years, where the work could be done on contract. If the Unification Church wanted some research done on the philosophy of religion, they might contract with the theology department of Bristol or Oxford to carry out the work for them.

I have taken examples from the arts subjects because it is in these areas that the system of contracts, especially private contracts, seems especially bizarre. And it is in fact obvious that when the idea was put forward, it was the sciences, and particularly the applied sciences, that the Government had in mind. There is an acknowledgement in the DES paper already quoted that difficulties may arise in connection with other subjects: 'The government has recognised that a system of contracting must be so designed as to avoid damage to aspects of the work of institutions, such as the advancement of learning, which cannot readily be embraced by specific contractual commitments.' In the light of this assurance, and in the absence, so far, of any clarification of the nature of the contractual relation proposed between funding councils and institutes of higher education, it is best perhaps to avoid detailed consideration of the topic. The whole idea may yet be forgotten.

Before leaving it entirely, however, some general reflexions may be appropriate. In the case of the polytechnics we saw that, if they are to revert at least partly to their intended role—that is, if they are to become centres of applied science and technology—the idea of contracts between them and industry, or between them and government departments is not wholly absurd, though this should never form more than a part of their funding. Both for specific short-term research, however, and for supplying training or retraining for an industrial work-force (including managers) a contract for the supply of a particular intellectual commodity might be an efficient way of proceeding. But even so it would be necessary to take precautions to ensure the continuity of the establishment and its proper commitment to basic research and teaching, as well as to immediate short-term results to be commissioned one by one.

The case of the universities is different. It cannot be held that the universities should dedicate themselves primarily to short-term research or specific training, however academically high-powered the new work-force is supposed to be. The passing reference in the White Paper to the advancement of learning, as though this were only a small part of what universities are devoted to, little more than a side-line, is not a sufficient acknowledgement of what is in fact their primary function, both in the sciences and the arts. Indeed there is a curious sense in which the authors of the White Paper, perhaps mainly arts-educated themselves, are blinded by science, to the extent of not really understanding what science is. There is a perpetual identification implied between science and technology, and an assumption that a university devoted entirely to this composite study would be serving best the needs of the country as a whole. If a bow is made to arts subjects it is mainly on the grounds that they are 'enriching'. Hardly a bow is made at all in the direction of the most abstract and theoretical subjects of all: mathematics, physics, and astronomy.

The second respect in which the new Funding Council differs from the old UGC is not disconnected from the first, and is more threatening from the point of view of the universities. The UGC, as has already been said, was established to be a buffer between universities and government. It was also intended to be a go-between. Not only did it carry out the intentions of government in the distribution of university funds, but it carried to government messages about university needs. While disinterested and as far as possible equitable between one university and another, it was nevertheless thought to be on the whole friendly to universities, and able to interpret and explain their needs to a possibly hostile Treasury. The new Council has no such role. The relation between the Council and government is defined in terms of the guidance it will receive from government on funding provisions, on the size and balance of the university system, and on specific policy developments. It will also receive a 'financial memorandum' setting out how its money will be allocated and how it should be transmitted to the universities. In addition, and as a matter of last resort, the Secretary of State may issue directions to the Council. The Council has no right to issue even suggestions to the Secretary of State. There is no doubt that the effect of this change is to bring the universities far more directly under the control of Whitehall, and of the Secretary of State personally.

I have argued already for the accountability of higher education both to Parliament and to society, and for the need to have a policy for higher education that is visibly a continuation of the policy for the rest of education. Education must be thought of as a continuum, and there is no case whatever for instituting changes in one sector (the schools) that is not reflected in the other sectors (higher and continuing education). Nevertheless the new arrangements appear to pay little or no attention to another principle that is equally valuable, that of academic freedom.

'Academic freedom' is a phrase that has been much used in the period since the Second World War, and has been used in a variety of totally different contexts. I do not believe that there is, or should be, such a thing as perfect or complete academic freedom, nor do I think that universities can justify extravagance or other bad practice in its name. But it is, all the same, a concept that cannot be neglected if the universities are to play the part they should in the education and culture of the country, as well as in the field of international science and learning. What should such freedom consist in? Is there a workable definition to be offered as a counterbalance to the manifest advantages of a coherent and centrally organized educational system? Is there a sense in which academic freedom can be recognized as a value worthy to be generally defended, not a cover-up for élitist abuses or inbuilt inertia?

It is easiest to think of academic freedom in terms of its most obvious opposite, the tyranny over the universities exercised by totalitarian governments; the rewriting of biology and history in the Soviet Union, the compulsion brought to bear on medical scientists in Nazi Germany to conduct research on eugenics and use Jews for this purpose. These are abuses of intellectual resources about which we are right to feel very strongly indeed; and the ideal, set against them, is that of a community of scientists and other academics, at liberty both to choose their own topics for research, and to follow their arguments and their discoveries wherever they may lead, even if the outcome is contrary to the ideology of a particular government. In this sense there can be no doubt that the freedom of the universities is an ideal to be pursued as surely as any other freedom from tyranny; and the tyranny over men's minds has always, rightly, seemed the worst and most terrible kind of all. Indeed there is a genuine contradiction between the idea of a university and the notion that what is taught should be subject to ideological constraints. The pursuit of truth must be the motive for the academic, even though he may often disclaim anything so grandiose, and be more interested in getting his book published, or getting better results for his students than his neighbours or rivals.

But this central ideal, the free pursuit of truth, does not entail that absolutely *any* subject must be taught at *all* universities, regardless of costs. It is concerned only with the content of what is taught, wherever that happens to be. Thus if there were only one university in the United Kingdom that taught history this, though odd, would not in itself be contrary to the spirit of academic freedom. All that would matter would be that at this sole university no pressure should be brought to bear on the department to limit the content and direction of the course for other than academic reasons. It hardly needs saying that freedom of thought is far more easily assured when there is a variety of different history faculties throughout the country. But this is not an essential requirement of freedom.

If academic freedom is essentially concerned with the freedom to follow research without ideological strings attached, and to teach whatever is the outcome of such research, and publish it in all other ways, then such freedom is not incompatible with the rationalization of research facilities, expensive equipment being shared between institutions; nor even with the removal from some universities of facilities for research in particular subjects, adequately covered elsewhere. To say that earth sciences should not be taught in every university is not to place restrictions of an ideological nature on the content of such earth sciences courses as remain.[12] In a time of general financial constraint, such rationalization must be accepted. Obviously it needs watching: a particular government might be inclined to close down this rather than that university department on account of the political non-acceptability of its output. It is easy to imagine the closure of a department concerned with, let us say, the risks attached to the civil uses of nuclear energy, by a government committed to the increased use of nuclear generating stations. But a *generally* free system with a strong tradition of peer-assessment, and channels through which government can be regularly advised, should take care of such dangers.

The cause of academic freedom is sometimes invoked to defend the system of 'tenure' in university posts. Tenure gives the incumbent of a particular position in a university—Senior Lecturer, Reader, or Professor—assurance that, once he has served an apprenticeship in a more junior position, he is secure until retiring age in his senior post. Such a system is widely regarded in Government circles as an abuse, and is cited as an explanation for the costliness and inefficiency with which universities are often charged.

The issue is not straightforward. In the first place it has to be remembered that even without official 'tenure', it is often extraordinarily difficult to remove an incompetent person from any job, except possibly in industry. To sack a schoolteacher except for gross misbehaviour is almost impossible, after his probationary year is over. Universities are not alone in being encumbered by some members of staff who ought not to be there. Moreover, tenure is often a matter of convention rather than law. Most college appointments in Oxford are for a term of years; but the renewal after each five- or seven-year period is generally regarded as a formality. Tenure is harder to achieve in the USA, and so there is more mobility, and more horse-trading, among academic staff. Yet in many American private schools, where appointments are on a one-year contract, it is almost unheard of for a contract not to be renewed.

Even if incompetence is a ground for removal it is extremely hard to prove incompetence in an academic field. The number of publications a person has to his credit is not a good criterion of competence; indeed, it is a disastrous test to apply, leading to the publication of innumerable bad books in all subjects. Asking the students, likewise, is a dubiously satisfactory way of testing for good teaching. A continuing genuine interest in his subject is what an academic above all needs to have; but, short of asking him, it may be hard to find out whether he has this.

However, there are reasons other than incompetence for making academic staff redundant, the major reason being that the university has decided it must close or diminish a particular department. It is manifestly absurd to keep academic staff if they have fewer and fewer pupils, undergraduate or graduate, and in the academic world of specialists and scholars it is impossible to think of 'retraining', and correspondingly hard to move sideways. There are academics who go into university administration. But it is very undesirable to keep administration and teaching wholly distinct. Nor is it good for a university to have as registrars or chairmen of committees only people who are at the top end of the age-scale, having given up their academic work. If removing tenure means leaving a university free to make redundant those academics who no longer have a genuine role in that university, then there is no doubt that tenure must go. Nor is there any reason at all to suppose that academic freedom in the serious sense will be thereby jeopardized. Of course, if an academic post is held only for a period of years and has to come up for periodic renewal, it is technically easier for an interventionist government to get a particular academic removed from his post. But it is in the last degree unlikely that intervention will be at this level. It must be assumed that universities will retain the rights to appoint whom they wish and retain their services, within reason, as long as they are needed.

However, although I have argued that some frequently expressed fears for academic freedom are misplaced, it will not do to be complacent. The two innovations with which I have been concerned, the system of contracts and the absence from the terms of reference for the new Funding Council of any statutory duty to advise Government, could, together, pose a genuine threat. As I have already suggested, a university department known to be working in a field where government has an interest in a particular outcome might not have its contract renewed. The department might then have to close and its staff be made redundant. And so inevitably we would begin to see control over the content of research (and teaching), not merely over its structure and location. The safeguard against this must be the vigilance of the universities; but, above all, their right to be heard through an official body with access to government, such as the UGC used to be in its early days. An amendment to the 1988 Education Reform Bill tabled by Lord Jenkins of Hillhead, the Chancellor of Oxford University, sought to ensure that individuals would not be removed from their posts on the grounds that they were putting forward unpopular or controversial views, and this amendment was carried. It is not certain whether the amendment will be incorporated in the Act; but, in any case, though partially reassuring, it is not enough to safeguard whole departments, which must also be thought of as able to exercise academic freedom. However that may be, academic freedom is an ideal we must value and cherish watchfully if we are to have any universities worth the name. If we are careless of it, if we exaggerate or invoke it unnecessarily in our defence, we shall end up with a set of government research establishments, and government-regulated teaching institutions. Even if, as I have suggested, expenditure on research has to be rationalized, facilities to some extent shared; even if, in some universities, earth sciences or, as it might be, nuclear physics has to go to be carried on elsewhere, it is essential that in every university there should be research in both arts and sciences, its content and subject matter determined by the academics who practise it, and joined in a close marriage with teaching departments.

It might be argued that, having allowed for the necessity of 'shared facilities', I have given away the case. If it is true that, in pursuit of economy and efficiency, not every university should be permitted to carry out research in every subject, why not complete the rationalization in the manner first proposed by the Advisory Board for the Research Councils?[13] They argued that universities should be distinguished into three levels: the R, the X, and the T. R level universities should devote themselves solely to research. These should become the centres of excellence for the sciences where the expensive resources would be concentrated. Below them in the pecking order would be run-of-the-mill universities, concerned with both research and undergraduate teaching, and with taught courses for graduates; finally there would be those universities that would be devoted almost wholly to teaching. It is unlikely that those who taught at these establishments would actually be forbidden to undertake research. But they would have no facilities and, presumably, a teaching load that would make scholarship an impossibility.

Such a tripartite division of the universities seems to me not merely to put excessive constraints on academic freedom, but actually to threaten the very existence of a large number of our universities. This is not the mere conservative objection to change which, it is frequently suggested, is all that those within the university system are capable of. It is rather that this particular change shows ignorance of what it is that universities are supposed to do. Nor is it in any way entailed by the argument that there must be a rationalization of resources in the establishing of centres for research.

There are two different ways in which such rationalization could be carried out. The simplest way would be to direct that some departments be closed and the staff moved to another university, where, in future, the resources would be concentrated. This might not be popular with any of the universities involved; but it would be possible, and perfectly compatible with the future status of the university stripped of its physics or astronomy or earth sciences. The second way would be to set up some research centres not part of any university, but used to some extent by all (or most), to which teams of scientists could be seconded for a period of years from their home university. Such establishments (rather like the Institute for Advanced Studies in Princeton) might attract distinguished foreign workers as well as natives, and arts scholars as well as scientists might come there to work for limited periods. Some research students would be supervised there, and there would be at least computerized distance access to all university libraries. Such an idea has attractions, and, though it would be initially expensive, might save money in the end. Neither of these schemes of rationalization would alter the character of the university sector as a whole. The second is particularly appealing, since it would open the way to greater cross-over between universities and polytechnics, whose members would also have access to the research institutes, or whatever the centres would be called. Even if it made sense to establish centres at, say, Cambridge, London, Oxford, or Warwick, and though there would be perhaps especially close collaboration between the centres and those universities, the nature of the universities themselves would not be radically changed by proximity to the institute, and it would be a matter of policy that research originating in other universities and polytechnics should also be pursued in the institutes.

What is essential to the whole future of education and learning is that no university should be altogether deprived of its freedom to engage in research, even if it is acknowledged that, in order to pursue advanced research in some particular field of knowledge, a scientist may have to go elsewhere. For the crucial distinction between Higher Education and other sorts of education simply is its connection with research, and whatever the exact nature of the binary line, this must be as true of polytechnics as of universities.

At school, sixth-form college, or college of further education (and indeed at the so-called colleges of higher education), however good a teacher you have, you are generally learning the 'received wisdom' in your subject. Your teacher may express his views on this wisdom, and his views may be critical or eccentric, but it is unlikely that he will himself be engaged in discovering new things, pushing out the frontiers of knowledge, or publishing objections to orthodox thinking. He is unlikely to have either time or research resources to enable him to enter new fields. Moreover, his task will be among other things to enable his students to pass examinations set and marked outside his own establishment, and based on the assumption of 'received' knowledge. At university and in the more independent polytechnics, on the other hand, the student will become aware of a profound difference. Even if not all of his teachers are themselves engaged in innovatory research, they may be presumed to be in touch with such research through colleagues. It is part of the experience of higher education that a student should realize that his teachers are as much devoted to their subject, understanding it and advancing it, as to their pupils. I do not deny that some teachers in higher education teach very badly, and this is a hardship for their pupils, and something that should be remedied as far as possible. But being a good teacher is not, and cannot be, the *whole* function of someone employed in higher education. This is indeed at the heart of the matter; it is what makes higher education 'higher'. For it has the consequence that a student in higher education is conscious of being on the edge of a developing world of learning. He may go to lectures or seminars where changes in his subject are not only discussed, but are being made there before his eyes and ears. The very syllabus he follows, although on paper it may be the same as last year and the year before, may, in practice, change quite radically during the three years he is at university to accommodate advances in a subject which, possibly, are being initiated on his own doorstep.

It is not possible to overestimate the importance of the research factor in universities and polytechnics from the standpoint of the students; and I am not talking only of exceptional or highly academic students, but of those who may in fact have no intention of engaging in research themselves. However students spend their time at university, whatever they go on to do thereafter, they will inadvertently have entered the world in which advances are made, revolutions in thought and in practice are started. They will come to realize how little is known, how much more there is to be discovered, and how infinite are the boundaries of their chosen subject. This is not simply a matter of sentiment; it is essential to the spirit of enterprise and free speculation without which a system of education is a mere luxury. If it is seriously proposed to remove all research facilities from some of our universities and make them into teaching establishments (where the students will inevitably be back as they were at school, at the centre; where *getting good grades for them* is the main object of their teachers), then at least let us ensure that such establishments are not called universities, or, for that matter, polytechnics. If there must be an institutionalized pecking order in post-school education, then let the lowest-grade institutions be given another name (colleges perhaps), let them give certificates or sub-degree diplomas only, and let no one suppose that students whose education comes to an end after attending such an institution have actually been exposed to higher education as it should be understood. There may be a demand for such colleges (and, as I have suggested already, they might well be useful in supplying access courses, working closely with universities and polytechnics) but they should not be thought of as a part of higher education itself.

Obviously there are already great differences between one university and another, one polytechnic and another. Some are better than others; some better in particular fields. But this is something that can be accommodated quite well in the system, just as can, within reason, differences between schools. It may well be, too, that there is a need to raise the general standard in higher education, as there is in the rest of education. What would be disastrous would be deliberately to encourage some institutions to aim at nothing but 'efficient teaching'. One may properly ask *what* are they supposed efficiently to teach? The answer must be 'arts and sciences at an elementary level'. As soon as that became clear, then the quality of the teachers and the students would settle at a low level, unlikely to be elevated by any of the trappings of a university, however faithfully preserved. It would be idle to pretend that these essentially 'liberal arts colleges' could command any general esteem, let alone parity of esteem with real universities and polytechnics. In a leading article in the *Times Higher Education Supplement* there was the following warning:

There is a lot of loose talk about liberal arts colleges in the United States designed to reassure those universities which may be wobbling at the end of the plank that the water is not really so very cold. Don't believe it. With the exception of a few well-known Colleges . . . and even they are a bit Scott Fitzgeraldy . . . [and, I would add, extremely rich] . . . American liberal arts colleges have academic standards that make the average British adult-education institute seem an intellectual power-house.[14]

Broadly I believe this is true. If fixed in a rigid and unalterable structure, the gap between our good universities and bad would widen and become incapable of being bridged; and this would be bad equally for our education and our international prestige.

I have argued that a whole system of education must contain provision for education up to a fixed age, before which attendance at school should be compulsory, and also for education after that age, for school-leavers, adults, and those who at various stages of their life will need training or retraining. In this respect it is essential that the whole system should be under scrutiny together, and a certain amount of central intervention may be necessary to establish a general direction that will satisfy the needs of society (including the needs of those to be educated) and will prevent costs running totally out of control. To some extent, then, higher education should not be outside the scope of government initiative or direction.

But there is a sense in which any central overview of education must recognize that at the top end, among the institutions of higher education, there must be a built-in independence to pursue learning and research wherever there is new work to be done in whatever field. If academic freedom is not recognized as a principle at this level there can be no life in the system lower down. To demand such independence (not absolute, but as a proper ideal) may seem like self-indulgence or arrogance. In the 1980s, when universities on the whole have a bad name, there is a tendency to wish to put them down, to let them take what's coming to them, to 'serve them right'. But to fulfil its function, higher education must be the source of questioning, critical, and sceptical minds. Students will acquire these attributes only if their teachers are free to pursue knowledge and learning wherever they have a passion to do so. Without these attributes, we shall not be in a position to find teachers, not just for universities and polytechnics, but for schools, where the need is greatest of all. To produce such teachers must be regarded as one of the main functions of higher education, just as important as the function of producing skilled technicians and managers. To overlook this has been one of the main mistakes of the last twenty or thirty years.

Good teachers will not emerge from universities or polytechnics that are not permitted to set standards of academic excellence. There can be no other source of new knowledge or scholarship and their dissemination than the universities and polytechnics themselves. Experience, skill, and judgement may come from the workshop and the class-room; but new discovery must come from the institution of higher education and research. However intensely government may desire to see these institutions become efficient and cost-effective, it cannot take *this* function of the universities to itself. It is here that the industrial analogy, with its contracts to turn out certain specifiable quality-controlled products, finally breaks down. It is the universities and polytechnics themselves that must set the criteria by which quality is to be judged.

Conslusion 6

I argued in the last chapter that universities and polytechnics, in different though overlapping spheres, must be free to conduct their own research within a reasonable financial framework, and that it will be fatal for higher education if its teaching and research functions become separate. But this is not a general argument for things to remain just as they are. Indeed, the condition of the educational system as a whole will not improve nor will its outcome be more satisfactory, without profound changes.

The first and most important change is that the theoretical and the practical should be recognized as the two great arms of the educational system and should replace as the central dichotomy within the curriculum that between the arts and the sciences. They should be recognized as of equal importance, and allowed to flourish side by side in the same schools. To say that in education we must learn to take the practical as seriously as the academic has become one of the major clichés of the 1980s. But we shall not begin to live up to this admirable precept until we have built the distinction, with equal weight given to each part, into the school curriculum and the examination system. And we shall not live up to it if we try to combine it with an old-fashioned demand for separate schools where only the academic shall be taught.

Within the sciences in particular we need to focus on the distinction between practice and theory, the applied and the 'pure'. It has long been recognized by some scientists that technical innovation does not automatically arise from advances in pure science. It is the applied sciences that are immediately responsive to the market. The demand for things that people can have and use, things that work and can then be sold, will always produce invention and creativity in the applied sciences.

Creativity and imagination in the pure sciences will in turn affect practical inventiveness, but only slowly and unpredictably. And so equal support for the pure and the applied is absolutely essential, and this must be reflected in the school curriculum and examination system, and in the distinct functions of the polytechnics and universities. It must be the polytechnics that work most closely with industry, acting both as extensions of the research and development wings of individual industries and as sources of training and retraining for those working within particular companies, and as that sector of higher education and research most readily able to respond to market demands.

Moreover—and this has been at the centre of my argument— the basic distinction between the practical and the theoretical is just as important in the arts as in the sciences, even if it is less familiar. The words 'pure', and 'applied', 'theoretical', and 'practical', are less apt in this field, and it may be that we should think of different terminology with which to draw the line. But however that may be, part of the cause of our national illiteracy has been that the distinction has been overlooked. Education has for years been too clerical, too much dependent on the written word. And so there are children who leave school unable to speak their own language with competence, let alone anyone else's. The half-baked confusion in teaching between the handing on of a cultural literary tradition and the use of language here and now for practical communication has done great harm not only to our competence but to our powers of accuracy and analysis. Literature and the other arts must be taught at school. Children must be given the chance to confront them and contribute to them, but recognizing them for what they are, sources of vast pleasure and insight, not instruments for the production of some measurable or necessarily marketable result.

At the same time, the 'theoretical' (or 'non-applied') in the case of both the arts and the sciences must become more critical and more philosophical than it is at present; and this will, I believe, have practical implications, albeit slow to appear. For the habit of standing back and comparing quite different things one with another, of analysing a phenomenon and imagining how it could be otherwise, of envisaging how things would be if this were not so (which may be called a 'philosophical' habit), is what is needed in innovation and good management, whether industrial, commercial, or social. Transferability of knowledge and skills, recognized as a mark of effective education, comes from the development of such powers of analysis and criticism, and the freedom they bring to escape from the actual into the possible and the future. Imagination and inventiveness ultimately spring from thus reinterpreting the 'theoretical'.

This kind of change of direction in the theoretical, going along with the explicit separation of the theoretical from the practical, must start at school and be built into the structure of the school curriculum. If this is to come about the major requirement is that there should be teachers who believe in it and who are capable of maintaining a clear vision of what they are teaching, and what they are teaching it for. The concepts of 'understanding' and 'being able to do' are now enshrined in the rubric of our new GCSE examinations. We need a new generation of teachers who will interpret these concepts in a realistic and imaginative way. The universities and polytechnics must supply such teachers; and it is of the utmost importance that this part of their function should be recognized and encouraged. We in the universities are often reproached for not sending the best undergraduates into industry. It is a far more serious matter for reproach that we do not send them into teaching. There are, as I have suggested, understandable reasons why people do not want to teach; but *that* they do not is, nevertheless, a failure in our educational policy.

We must develop a policy that embraces all of education, from primary schools to polytechnics and universities, so that, thinking of the system as one, we may learn to think of no one part of it as more important, or more chic, than another. Primary schools must influence secondary by sending on pupils who are alert and ready, and with some graded tests under their belts, indicating what they can do and like doing as well as what they know. Secondary schools must influence establishments of higher education, sending on to them pupils who are ready, thoughtful, and creative, with a variety of accomplishments, theoretical and practical, of which they will have intelligible records in the form of test results. In such an atmosphere of mutual influence and respect, teachers will be forthcoming who will be willing (for decent reward) to go back into the system at whatever level their greatest expertise and interest may lie. In this sense our educational policy needs to be common.

There is another way in which a common policy is even more important. If we really believe that the practical and techno-logical is as important as the intellectual and theoretical, and if we genuinely want to improve the educational output of our schools and universities, we must believe that education is for everybody, not just for an élite of clerks and academics. It is essential that our education policy should be one that is to the advantage of everybody, all children, all students, all those who need or want to come back into education. I have argued that the system of provision through comprehensive schools (with or without a parallel system of independent schools) followed by a variety of different kinds of further and higher education is the most effective system to carry out such a common policy. And this was primarily an educational argument. There is also, however, a fundamental political point to be made.

An educational policy that is for *everyone* is not necessarily one that is incompatible with competition. Within schools pupils may compete to do better than their fellows and win the still-glittering prizes. Schools may compete with one another to do better for their pupils. But if competition has emerged, by the third term of the Conservative Government, as the central That-cherite concept, then we must remember that competition can best and most fruitfully take place in a condition of justice, where everyone may enter the race and do his best. In the days of selective education it came to be realized that those who were not selected at 11 + could not enter the competition. Therefore they had virtually no chance at all of winning. To go back to a system of 'special' schools, whether these are called grammar schools or technical colleges or 'grant-maintained' schools (having opted out, that is from Local Authority control), is in effect to go back to a time when the 'ordinary' schools educated children who could not enter the race. The more powerful the spirit of Thatcherite free enterprise, the less acceptable this preselection will become. Once we saw through the pretence of the 11 + examination to be a fair and equitable means of selection, we realized that we wanted a system within which the competition itself was fair and not biased in favour of a minority. In a similar way, at the end of the century, if we all want to be middle-class, if we are all upwardly mobile, it is not politically realistic to cut off some children at 11 from the mobility stakes.

In August 1987 a Mori opinion poll was carried out among parents to ascertain the kind of schools they wanted. A large majority of them came out in favour of a return to grammar schools. On the other hand, a mere handful were in favour of selection at 11. It was only this handful, one must presume, who realized that it is impossible to have grammar schools without selection. It seems to me that there are two lessons to be learned from this poll. First, parents want *better* schools for their children, schools where they will be taught what they need to know if they are to get on in the world; and, understandably, these same parents think of the grammar school as fulfilling this role. On the other hand, they want everyone to have the benefit of such schools: they don't want to go back to the injustice of an examination which condemned a majority of children to 'worse' schools.

The second lesson is more significant. Parents, whether they are asked to give their answers to a questionnaire or are faced with an actual choice of school for their children, will consider only their own children and what they think best for them— quite properly since they are being given a choice in their capacity as parents. But even if every set of parents in the country gave the same answer, that they would prefer a grammar school, that would not necessarily mean that the Government should adopt the policy of reintroducing grammar shools. It is the role of government, as it is not of individual parents, to think of the whole. All the parts do not add up to the whole in such a case as this. Paramount among the considerations of a government committed to improving the welfare of the whole country through education must be the avoidance of educational waste. The government must therefore consider how to avoid wasting teachers and the talents of pupils who, with free parental choice, would be relegated to the 'left-over' schools, after parents had chosen their preferred schools. The parents making the choices, real or hypothetical, do not have to bother with such problems. They simply have to choose what they personally and from their own narrow viewpoint regard as the best. It is essentially the role of government to see further than this understandable kind of myopia allows.

If Local Authorities are no longer to be trusted to look after the educational well-being of all their constituent pupils (and obviously the more schools choose to free themselves from Local Authority control, the less universal that control can be), then to look after all must be the task of central government. A common national curriculum has been the first step. A stated common policy for all schools, colleges, polytechnics, and universities would be the next. Provided those involved in research, the writing of textbooks, the setting of examination papers, and the producing of educational broadcasting are totally free with regard to the content of their material, there is no harm in such a centralized system. It would be overtly paternalistic. But paternalism, though no doubt potentially dangerous, is not necessarily harmful. It may lead people in directions they are too ignorant or too short-sighted to discover for themselves. Above all, paternalism may have in mind that old but by no means outworn concept, the Common Good. The educational system must get its content and its inspiration ultimately from the new knowledge that will come from the polytechnics and the universities, and from the professionals in the class-room, interpreting and delivering this knowledge. But its form must come from outside. No one has the authority to impose form on the educational system but Parliament itself. It is crucial, therefore, that Parliament should base its decisions not on prejudice or ignorance, but on a democratic belief in the possibility of educating all children. Such a belief requires both imagination and hope. But without these virtues there can be no education.

References

Chapter 1

1. *Children and their Primary Schools* (HMSO, 1967), sect. 2, para. 9.
2. Ibid., para. 505.
3. John Dewey, *Democracy and Education* (New York: Macmillan, 1966).
4. See *Ruskin Plus Ten* (University of Exeter, 1986).
5. G. Cooke and P. Gosden, *Education Committees* (London: Councils and Education Press, 1986).

Chapter 2

1. Michael Oakeshott, 'Education: the Engagement and its Frustrations', in R. F. Deardon, P. Hirst, and R. S. Peters (eds.), *Education and the Development of Reason* (London: Routledge and Kegan Paul, 1972).
2. John Wilson, 'Integration of the Maladjusted', in J. Loring and G. Baron (eds.), *The Integration of Handicapped Children in Society* (London: Routledge and Kegan Paul, 1972). Much of the same flavour is to be found in the same author's *Philosophy and Practical Education* (London: Routledge and Kegan Paul, 1978).
3. Eric Midwinter, *Projections: an educational priority area at work* (London: Ward Lock, 1972).
4. *A Survey of the Teaching of A Level English Literature in 20 Mixed Sixth Forms in Comprehensive Schools* (DES, 1987).
5. See the report on *The Teaching of English in Schools* (the Kingham report) (HMSO, 1988). The report, though useful, seems to me to perpetuate a dangerous confusion between 'knowing about language' and 'knowing language', that is, being able to use it.
6. *A New Choice of School* (DES, 1987).
7. DES Command Document 9469, 1986.

Chapter 3

1. Edmund Holmes, *What Is and What Might Be* (London: Constable, 1911).

2. *Observer*, 23 August 1987.
3. Patricia Broadfoot, 'Alternatives to Public Examinations', in Desmond L. Nuttall (ed.), *Assessing Educational Achievement* (Falmer Press, 1986).
4. *Curriculum and Examinations in Secondary Schools* (HMSO, 1943).
5. *Fifteen to Eighteen* (HMSO, 1959).
6. Tim Horton, 'Course-work', in Tim Horton (ed.), *GCSE: examining the new system* (New York: Harper & Row, 1986).
7. Ian McNay, 'GCSE and the New Vocationalism', in Horton, op. cit.
8. The GOML (Graded Objectives in Modern Languages) initiative started in the mid-1970s.

Chapter 4

1. *Whose Schools? A Radical Manifesto* (London: Hillgate Group, 1986), p. 15.
2. Ibid., p. 10.
3. *The Times*, 28 May 1987.
4. R. S. Peters, *Education and Ethics* (London: Allen and Unwin, 1966).
5. See *Times Educational Supplement*, 5 June 1987.
6. *Quality in Schools: the Initial Training of Teachers* (HMSO, 1987).
7. Ibid., p. 14.
8. Ibid., p. 114.
9. See *The Internship Scheme: an Information Pack for Schools* (Oxford University Department of Educational Studies, January 1987).

Chapter 5

1. DES Statistical Bulletin, April 1987.
2. Higher Education Report of the Committee on Higher Education under the chairmanship of Lord Robbins (HMSO Command Paper 2154, 1963).
3. *Listener*, 30 January 1986.
4. *Times Higher Education Supplement*, 10 July 1987.
5. *Higher Education: Meeting the Challenge* (HMSO, 1987), para. 2.20.
6. Pat Fleetwood-Walker and Peter Taylor, 'Jam Today', in Colin Titmus (ed.), *Widening the Field: Continuing Education in Higher Education* (Open University Press, 1987).
7. Tyrrell Burgess, third essay in Titmus, op. cit.
8. Thomas Rohlen, *Japan's High Schools* (University of California Press, 1983).

9. Ibid., para. 4. 11.
10. See the debate in the House of Lords, 22 July 1987 (Hansard).
11. *Changes in Structure and National Planning for Higher Education: Universities Funding Council* (DES, 1987).
12. See *Strengthening University Earth Sciences: Report of a Committee chaired by Professor E. R. Oxburgh* (UGC, 1987).
13. *A Strategy for the Science Base* (Advisory Board for the Research Councils, 1987).
14. *Times Higher Education Supplement*, 22 May 1987.

Index

Index compiled by Peva Keane